Find the Power to Escape Your Past

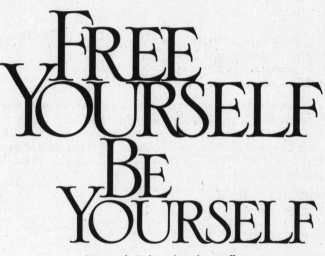

FREE YOURSELF BE YOURSELF

Previously Released as *Shame Off You*

ALAN D. WRIGHT

MULTNOMAH
BOOKS

FREE YOURSELF, BE YOURSELF
PUBLISHED BY MULTNOMAH BOOKS
12265 Oracle Boulevard, Suite 200
Colorado Springs, Colorado 80921

ISBN 978-1-60142-276-7
ISBN 978-0-307-56326-2 (electronic)

Published in the United States by WaterBrook Multnomah, an imprint of the Crown Publishing Group, a division of Random House Inc., New York.

MULTNOMAH and its mountain colophon are registered trademarks of Random House Inc.

Cataloging-in-Publication data is on file with the Library of Congress.

Printed in the United States of America
2010

10 9 8 7 6 5 4 3 2 1

SPECIAL SALES
Most WaterBrook Multnomah books are available at special quantity discounts when purchased in bulk by corporations, organizations, and special-interest groups. Custom imprinting or excerpting can also be done to fit special needs. For information, please e-mail SpecialMarkets@WaterBrookMultnomah.com or call 1-800-603-7051.

To my children:
May you soar to great heights
in the certainty of my love,
never in search of it.

For Abigail,
her father's joy:
I love you more than a million
Ghirardelli hot fudge sundaes.

and

For Bennett,
his father's blessing:
I love your sixty-yard sand wedge hole outs,
art masterpieces, and excellent schoolwork.
But I love you—just you—a million times more.

contents

acknowledgments

My thanks to:

Anne, my love. Aren't we blessed that, instead of my shame snuffing you out, your grace lit me up? Thanks for the depth of love that comes with two decades of marriage and for blessing me to write another book.

Jim Glasgow, Pastor "Gem." When, upon completion of your doctorate in ministry so many years ago, your child retorted to a friend, "My dad is a doctor, but not the kind that can help anybody," she was wrong. You've doctored my soul a thousand times. You're one of the best doctors in the world and I love you.

Mickey Thigpen. I'm pretty sure I'd lay my life down for you. I'm positive you've already laid yours down for me. Its not your intelligence, your work ethic, your theological insight, your humor, or your skill at running the church that I love about you most—it's your heart.

Katherine Currie. You are extraordinary. Ordinary people would become self-absorbed in your circumstances, but you have not turned inward with anxiety—you have turned outward with love. Thanks for giving Alan Wright Ministries the time that you did not have so that more people could discover God's love.

Bob Roach. Elder, pilot, mentor, friend, brother, promoter, planner, giver, and, when needed, rump kicker. Thanks for having the skill to fly this message around the nation, but thanks more for having the heart.

Reynolda elders. Your partnership in the gospel is a delight.

Pastor's Prayer Partners. As God breathes out blessing upon those who read these pages, it's because He first breathed in the incense of your intercession.

Reynolda Presbyterian Church. Oh, your hunger for the Word! Every weekend I feel like a grandmother smiling to see her Thanksgiving feast gobbled up by her hungry family.

Dudley Hall. The reason I had to write this book is because I couldn't package up you and send you to bookstores around the world. Whatever good can be read in these pages can already be seen more clearly in your life. Thanks so much for spiritually fathering me.

Don Jacobson. Phone calls with you are not chats, they are God moments. Thanks for letting me partner with Multnomah again.

Larry Libby. Man, you've got style! Thanks for capturing my heart and helping it beat more vividly on these pages.

foreword
by gary chapman

all of us have a history, and all of us have a future. We cannot change the past, but we can create our future. For most of us, our past is a mixed bag—some good memories and some painful memories. We have made some wise choices and some poor choices. We have been treated kindly by some people and have been abused by others. The experiences of the past speak to us every day. Some days, we hear, "You're appreciated; you made the right decision; you have many friends and great potential." Other days, we hear, "No one loves you; you are a loser; you will never amount to anything; you have no future."

How we respond to these voices from the past will determine our future. As a counselor, I have listened as people have told me of their distressing past. They speak of verbal, physical, and sexual abuse. They feel hurt, anger, and shame. On the one hand, they blame the people who hurt them, and on the other hand, they wallow in self-condemnation. Some have lived in the bondage of resentment and have sought to take revenge on those who have hurt them. The road of revenge has led some to atrocious acts of violence in an effort to "make them pay" for their wrongs. Others have turned their anger toward themselves. They blame themselves for all that has happened to them. They dress themselves in cloaks of shame and live behind emotional sunglasses, afraid to let anyone know who they really are. They reason that "No one would love me if they really knew me."

We were not created to live under cloaks of shame. The wonderful message from God is that He loves us and wants to heal our past, put His Spirit within us, and lead us into a fruitful future. With those who have sinned against us, God will be the judge. He is committed to justice and mercy. If they repent, God will forgive them. If they do not repent, God will judge them. We can release them and our hurt and anger into the hands of a loving and just God. We can breathe deeply and walk into the future freed from the pain of the past.

If you have pronounced judgment upon yourself for past failures or abuses, and imposed the sentence of misery upon your soul, God reminds you that Christ has already paid your penalty. You are free to walk out of jail and experience the freedom of release. The sun is shining. The flowers are blooming. You are free to enjoy the beauty of walking with God.

In this book, Alan Wright will share with you the details of how to experience freedom from shame and how to release your enemies to God. What you are about to read will show you how to *free* yourself to *be* yourself. God made you in His image. That image will be revealed as you lay aside the clothes of self-condemnation and blame and put on the clothes of forgiveness, kindness, and love. I predict that as you read and apply the principles in this book, you will discover your true self—the person God made you to be.

And I think you're going to love the person you discover.

—GARY CHAPMAN, author of *The Five Love Languages*
and *Love as a Way of Life*

CHAPTER ONE

COUP D'état

today is the anniversary of Saddam Hussein's execution.

Not so very long ago, his birthday was the most celebrated day on the Iraqi calendar. Now, however, the ousted, humbled, and imprisoned dictator has been tried, sentenced, and hung by the judicial system of a liberated and democratic Iraq. For several years, there has been no summoning of the citizenry to the mandatory birthday festivities.

With the former Baathist strongman's execution for crimes against humanity, more and more Iraqi citizens have come forward with tales of cruelty and torture at the hands of the former regime.

For some reason, the stories from the Iraqi national soccer team grieved me more than the rest. Once the athletes were speaking freely, we learned that they were severely punished if they didn't win. Before each game, Uday, Saddam's elder son, would call the team captain with threats of imprisonment—or worse—if they lost.

"The players would start crying," said Emmanuel Baba, a team member. "They would tremble with fear."[1]

Players told of being flogged, imprisoned, and put to forced labor in the wake of losing important games. They dared not quit the team for fear of being executed. One of the star players, Laith Hussein, confessed: "I thought many times of leaving soccer, but how could I? I was afraid of what Uday would do to me and my family. I would sit and cry when I was by myself. I want to play soccer for myself and the Iraqi people, not for Uday."

The soccer players' testimonies grip me so painfully because, in the first place, their suffering was linked to a game. A *game!* A game that kids play in their backyards. A game invented for only one end…fun. Life under an oppressive regime is hard enough. But when even the games become venues for punishment, it seems that humanity has sunk to its lowest ebb.

Upon further reflection, I must admit that the grief I feel while reading about the weeping soccer players runs deeper than my compassion for the abused athletes. I realize that I grieve for myself. On the one hand, the Iraqi oppression is a million miles away. An alien culture. A distant drama.

On the other hand, it is the story of my own soul.

the dictator within

I've had many successes in my life. But what has motivated my efforts for victory? The fun of the game, or the fear of punishment if I don't win? Have my accomplishments been fueled by the fulfillment I feel when I use my gifts well, or by the tyrannical threat to my self-worth if I don't always come out on top? Have I repeatedly entered life's field of endeavor to play for myself and the kingdom I represent, or has it been for a hidden, inward Uday calling before each game with his threats?

My answers to those self-inventory questions were laid bare one evening when I was enjoying bedtime prayers with my eight-year-old boy. I couldn't believe my ears when Bennett told God what he was thankful for that night. The next day was to be a big day for the boy—he was going to take his first academic tests. Because we'd been homeschooling Bennett for his second grade year, he hadn't been taking exams in traditional school fashion. So in keeping with our state law, we had contracted with an independent expert to test our son's scholastic aptitude.

I'm an unlikely homeschool parent because I spent my whole educational life maneuvering successfully in the traditional school system. I discovered early on that I could do well on tests. And it felt wonderful to excel. I not only wanted to make A's; I wanted to make "100s." I didn't want to make a great score; I wanted to make the *best* score. What started as a feeling of satisfaction over a job well done became a growing internal pressure to always be the best in the class. Anything less than an A would silently sting my soul. So I studied as much as necessary to ensure those top marks.

I loved those A's. My first semester at the University of North Carolina at Chapel Hill, I made straight A's. My dad wrote me at the end of that semester, expressing his pride in my accomplishment. I've kept that note for twenty-four years.

Though I loved making good grades, I didn't like tests. Tests were the cause of my late-night cramming sessions, churning stomach, and general dread. Life was always a matter of getting done with the tests. I always thought that life would begin for me when I had finished all my exams.

So there I knelt, the lifelong grade-fanatic of a dad, next to an eight-year-old boy who had never taken an academic test in his life. If you've ever felt an undue inward pressure to perform or the fear of possible failure at an upcoming exam, you'll understand why my boy's innocent prayer moved me so deeply.

"Lord, I'm thankful for all the fun things we did today, and God," Bennett prayed sincerely, "thank You that tomorrow the man is coming to our house and I get to take those tests."

I hid my tears so as not to confuse the lad who had prayed the golden prayer. I wept for joy because my boy was not afraid. No, more than that. I wept because I realized that my boy was learning for the sheer fun of learning, not for the tyranny of a test. It reminded me that there is a way to live apart from the pressure to perform. It filled me with joy to realize that my life-long oppressor had found no hold on my child.

Oh what sweet freedom is this! I wondered as I wiped my eyes. *What delicious liberty fills this boy's heart.*

Will you allow me one unadulterated parental boast? Second-grader Bennett, the examiner told us, tested as high as seventh grade level and no lower than fourth grade. How could it be? With no fear, no cramming, no late-night caffeine, my boy was outperforming the best I had ever brought to the classroom tests of my childhood!

There are two motives that can make a soccer player try hard—the fear of Uday or the fun of the game. There are two motives that can make a boy learn—the fear of the test or the thrill of discovery. There are two motives for succeeding in life—the fear of falling short or the faith that flies high.

It's just about that simple.

Life motivators

All people who try hard at life do so for one of two reasons—they're fearful and looking for acceptance, or they're fulfilled and looking to make a difference.

COUP D'ÉTAT | 15

These opposing life motivators are matters of the heart and can be well hidden from public view. This silent tyranny in my life wasn't revealed to me until I really wanted to improve my life. An honest inventory of my strengths and weaknesses revealed some recurring problems in my character that led me to some hard questions.

Here's the unvarnished truth. I, Alan Wright, couldn't bear even the mildest criticisms. As a result, I usually overreacted, justifying myself in the process or feeling a disproportionate weight of guilt. I tended to hear innocent questions or comments as criticisms. My wife's "the garbage needs to go out" sounded to me like "you're slacking." If she said, "the kids really have missed you this week while you were away" it sounded to me like "you're a bad father." *Why was I so sensitive to anything resembling criticism?*

I discovered mixed motives behind even my best efforts. Even when I was at my best, preaching well, helping someone in a crisis, or reaching out to a lonely person, I had to wonder, *Am I just doing this to help my church be successful so I will be a successful pastor and feel good about myself?*

I had difficulty speaking direct truth to people. Instead, I spent enormous energy behind the scenes trying to smooth things over or remove a person from a church leadership position without actually confronting the individual. That left me not only feeling phony, but also tired and often ineffective as a leader. *Why did I need everyone to like me?*

When I wanted my wife to change, I pointed out her deficiencies instead of encouraging her in all her strengths. We're in our twentieth year of marriage now and I'm happier than ever, but it took me a long time to see what I was doing. In the first years of marriage, I wasn't satisfied with her housekeeping. Then, for years after that, I wanted her to be more fit. In the early years of pastoring, I put pressure on her to be at church events because "what would people think" if the pastor's wife wasn't there? Anybody would tell you, Anne is a marvel—a joyous, beautiful, gifted woman. *With such a log in my own eye, why was I pointing out the specks in hers?*

I felt unduly doomed by my failures. I remember once getting a speeding ticket and, after the officer left I just sat in my car, shell-shocked and stunned, as if I had just committed a heinous crime. If I preached a bad sermon or we had poor attendance at church, I secretly worried about it. I was driven to succeed. Any other possibility elicited unadulterated dread. *Why couldn't I fail without feeling like a failure?*

I had a hard time keeping a sense of balance in my life. I caused a lot of stress in our marriage because I became so consumed with ministry. I felt like I had to say yes to every request for my help. Sometimes it seemed like everyone had access to my time except my own family. *Why did I have such vague boundaries in my life?*

I felt overly responsible for others' burdens. When I took clinical pastoral education in seminary and served each week as a hospital chaplain, I came home with awful headaches. When the doctor tested me and determined that I had no physiological problem, I had to admit that I was coming home from the hospital with all the patients' problems attached to me. I remember trying to watch a TV show with my wife at home one evening and thinking, "How can I sit here and enjoy this show while all those people are down at the hospital suffering so?" *Why couldn't I care for others without having to take on the weight of the world?*

I turned down honors and gifts. I know this may sound inconceivably stupid, but I was offered a full scholarship to seminary, a prize offered to only one incoming student. It would have paid everything. But I turned it down because I thought someone else "might need it more." On another occasion while in seminary, I preached at a nearby church one Sunday and was approached by a wealthy man in that congregation. He told me that he felt led to pay for my seminary. Further, he would like to help launch me into ministry the way he had helped another nationally known preacher.

I turned down both his offers.

How dumb can you get? What was wrong with me? *Was I really being nobly humble, or did I unconsciously think I didn't deserve such gifts and honors?*

Though I never fell into outright addiction, I felt its continual pull. I don't know how I managed to keep myself out of the snare. Partly fear, I suppose. I wouldn't let myself get swept away with pornography or sexual addiction because I feared it would cost me my ministry. I feared alcohol addiction because it was a family wrecker in my childhood home. I might have become fully addicted to my work if I didn't fear my wife abandoning me. *Why did I have to rely on fear to keep me from addictive behavior?*

Though I was successful, I often felt like an imposter. When I was a freshman in college, I took an honors section of a religion course. I never spoke out loud in the discussion class. After the first exam, the professor wrote on my paper, "Alan, anyone who can write an exam like this—nearly flawless work—really ought to speak out in class." Even then, I thought, *I'm not as smart as you think.*

Even as senior pastor of a vital church, I tended to think, "What am I doing in this position? Someone else could do a better job." When others lauded me, I often thought, "Yeah, but I'm not really as good as you think." *Why didn't it ever occur to me that maybe God HAD given me some important gifts and I DID have something special to offer?*

I felt held back from true greatness. I knew I could succeed, but only to a point. I had a gnawing sense that I would never fulfill my destiny until I felt differently about myself. As a kid, I played tennis and was ranked as high as twelfth in North Carolina, but I could never imagine myself being the best. I could see myself being really good at a lot of things, but I couldn't imagine myself becoming great.

I remember watching former Chicago Bulls great Michael Jordan when the game was on the line. He *wanted* the ball in his hands at the last second because he believed in his own greatness. Not me. I never wanted the ball in my hands for the last shot. At that last second, I would be too prone to think about the misery of shooting an air ball instead of the euphoria of swishing the net. It all left me wondering, *Is there something in me that shies away from ultimate success?*

sweet freedom

I now know the answer to those questions. I now know the root of my problems.

It's called shame.

Simply put, shame is a feeling of being inwardly flawed—of not measuring up. It probably sneaked into my soul back in fourth grade, when my family broke up. I became introverted and didn't talk about how embarrassed I was to be in a family besieged by alcoholism and divorce. I felt best about myself when I performed well, but never felt I performed *well enough*. Knowing you have to measure up in order to feel acceptable while knowing that you can't quite measure up leaves you with a gnawing anxiety that wreaks havoc in your soul.

These pages are, in large part, the memoirs of my coup d'état. Unlike Saddam, Shame is a tyrant that has no mustache, no giant statues of himself on display, and no portraits on every street corner. In fact, this tyrant prefers to remain in hiding and to rule undercover. For most of my life, I didn't even know it was there, hiding in my soul, silently dictating the direction of so many of my thoughts and emotions.

I'm pleased to report that Shame has been overthrown and Grace has become the main motivator in my life. But like anyone in a newly emancipated land, I still face skirmishes with the enemy. And I'm still discovering how to live as a newly liberated citizen.

I can't promise you that this freedom from shame comes easily or automatically, but I can promise you that real freedom is available.

And that it's sweet.

Sweeter than anything I've ever tasted.

You know how you feel after you've been successful? Everyone smiles and applauds your performance. No one berates you, no one shames or pressures you. Isn't the bliss of pure acceptance sweet? Can you imagine feeling like that all the time? Would you be shocked if I told you that's what life is supposed to feel like?

Imagine being able to laugh when you fall instead of looking around to see who else is laughing. Imagine failure becoming a teacher to instruct you rather than a ghost to haunt you. Imagine the deep, vague anxiety in your gut becoming a cool, quiet satisfaction instead. Imagine having no need to put others down because you feel so good about yourself. Imagine being able to enjoy your friends, your family, and your spouse instead of relegating them to the back burner in order to pursue your next accomplishment. Imagine feeling no terror at the thought of baring your soul to a confidant. Imagine the return of a real belly laugh. Imagine your thirst for booze, the adult channel, the shopping binge, or whatever numbs your hidden anxiety gone, quenched by a stream of living mercy.

I write because I have spent years studying the oppressive regime of shame in the souls of men and women. I want to expose this no good dictator for what it is—a vaporous liar that rules by fear. We will expose the anatomy of shame, dissecting it piece by piece. When you see it and understand it, you'll say not only, "I can't believe I've been motivated by that monster," but, "I want to be free!"

And free you can be. I promise—because God promises that "the truth will set you free." We need fresh explanations of the truth to correct our thinking, and we also need stories to touch our hearts and heal our wounds. The pages that follow offer more than an explanation of psychological principles; they offer the real stories of those set free by a transcendent Love. Stories of ordinary people like you and me.

Some of these ordinary lives are set in the landscape of the Bible. Some in my parish or home. Though I must reveal the emotional and mental dynamics of shame, I pledge to avoid getting lost in psychological technicalities. In fact, I pledge to do what I love most—tell my favorite love story.

I ask this of you. Be open-minded. Most people don't think they have shame issues, but all people do to some extent. Your shame may have some of the classic roots—broken home, alcoholic parent, abuse, molestation, performance pressure, conditional love. Or you may have simply breathed in shame like secondhand smoke from the polluted atmosphere of a fallen world. After all, shame is not only the tool of parents. Shame is everywhere and has been used in every setting—teachers, coaches, friends, employers, neighbors, And sadly, perhaps most profusely, preachers.

Please don't think your shame is too deep for anyone to understand. No matter how deep your wound, there's hope for healing in the pages to come. And please don't think your shame is so light that it should be ignored. Discovering these truths may mean the difference in living life halfheartedly and living life abundantly.

Though I write from the perspective of a follower of Jesus Christ, you don't have to be a Christian to benefit from what I have to say. Just understanding what motivates you will help you to change. Knowing your enemy's tactics will help you to defeat him. So regardless of your faith perspective, be assured that I do not write about shame in order to shame you into believing as I do. That said, if I am to be of any benefit to you, I must be transparent enough to show you how my soul is being healed. Ultimately, I have no healing mysteries to share but those that are plainly revealed in the Lover of my soul, Jesus Christ. Ultimately, I have no empowering gift to offer but the living presence of God's Spirit, who daily bathes me in grace.

What is your master motive? For whom do you perform? Joy

or Uday? It's time for your coup d'état. Time to change your motive for success. Time to play the soccer match because it's fun, not because you're scared. Time to *enjoy* excellence instead of striving for it. Join me for a magnificent journey from fear to fulfillment. From hidden pressure to hidden peace. Though others have tried to motivate you with the refrain "Shame on you," I'm here with a new command: "Shame off you!"

ASK   A Question to Inquire:

What motivates my efforts for victory—the fear of failure or the fullness of self-worth?

BELIEVE   A Principle to Ponder:

"Every person who tries hard at life does so for one of two reasons—he's fearful and looking for acceptance or he's fulfilled and looking to make a difference."

I do not need fear to motivate me for God has not given me a spirit that makes me "a slave again to fear, [for I have] received the Spirit of sonship" (Romans 8:15).

CHOOSE   A Commitment to Keep:

I choose today to uncover shame's influence in my life and commit myself to overthrow its silent tyranny in my soul.

PRAY

O God, You have promised that hidden things
will be exposed. Be the Light of Life to me now.
Fill my heart with Your shining grace, and reveal the shame
that hides in the shadows of my soul.
I long for the freedom of a shame-free life, so I offer
You full access to my heart and mind. Guide me on
this healing journey, and lead me into more abundant life.
In Jesus' name, AMEN.

when shame becomes grace

One glance and I knew she was a bruised reed.

Her hand trembled like a leaf when I met her for the first time. One more stiff wind and this fragile reed could snap. A *bruised reed He will not break*, I thought, and smiled. I knew there was hope for this woman. There's *always* hope. But what has happened in Grace McCracken's life is beyond what she, or anyone, could have hoped or imagined.

I couldn't have known how bruised a reed she was. Her bruises were formed early. Having presumed her childhood family to be a happy one, Grace's eight-year-old world was shredded when her dad left home. I don't know what an eight-year-old feels when her dad leaves.

But I know what it's like when you're ten.

Grace said she felt what I had felt. In her conscious reasoning, it wasn't her fault. But beneath the soul's veil hid an assumption: *I wasn't good enough to make them want to stay together*.

A broken home always breaks a child's heart. Always. And

now, sociologists tell us, nearly half of all American homes will be broken.

I don't know what a rejected wife feels either. I've counseled many. I've wept with them, prayed with them, and watched their souls bleed. But what's it like for a broken woman to raise a family with no money, no redeeming hope, and no source of limitless love? I can't imagine.

Grace's mom moved the family in with her own mother and stepfather, who themselves were in emotional pain. Grace's grandparents drank...and she never brought friends home to play at her house.

Until she was eight, Grace had never seen her strong-willed mother cry. So the day her mother broke down and openly wept before her children was imprinted on Grace's memory. So were her mother's words: *"If you children don't behave, I just don't know if I can raise you all."* Any eight-year-old could infer what it meant. *If you don't act the way I want you to act, you might not have your mother anymore.*

Parents often take away privileges as a means of discipline. It can be a constructive form of discipline to take away a kid's TV privileges or a teenager's car keys. But what every child fears losing more than anything else is a parent's love. Hurting parents sometimes step across an invisible line and instead of using discipline as an expression of their love, they dangle their love as an incentive. *You must behave better before I will give you my unfettered love. You must perform better before I will assure you that I accept you.* Most parents have no idea of the diabolical depths of what they are doing. The tactic works—on the surface. A child will do about anything to win a parent's love and acceptance.

What would you do for love?

That day, that heart-wrenching day when her mother shed tears, eight-year-old Grace McCracken made an inner vow. That vow became a foothold for dark forces in her life for the next forty years.

an impossible vow

Though the pledge that little girl made that day might have sounded noble, it was an oath conjured in hell. *"I will never let my mother cry again—I'll make sure she is always happy."*

Millions of us, unconsciously, have made similar oaths: *I must make others happy—or else they will not accept me.* From the day of her silent oath as a child, until the week after I met her, Grace McCracken had devoted her life to making her mother happy and winning her love. But love isn't always something that can be won. It must be a gift.

And Grace's mother never did become happy.

So Grace decided to work harder. When her aging mother had heart surgery and came to live with Grace and her husband, Grace saw it as another chance to succeed as a daughter. So she made a second oath: *No matter what, I will not let my mother die.* Obsessively, compulsively, Grace sought to be the perfect daughter. Despite giving her all, Grace could not save her mother's life. And when Grace's mother died, hope died inside of Grace.

Her soul was crippled with fear. She knew there was a deep gap between the person she had vowed to become and the person she perceived herself to be. That gulf was the source of her anxiety. Shame finds its foothold in that fault line—between what you *ought* to be and what you *are*. Unresolved, it's a chasm that invites a demonic mantra of despair: *You must measure up to be worth anything, but you can't measure up, so what's the use in living?* It was an anxiety that at times paralyzed her with "what ifs" and over time turned inward to form a suffocating, seemingly incurable depression.

Shame binds people into a prison of performance-based living. I believe shame to be the single greatest source of anxiety in the universe. It ruins lives and ravages families. Some live with low levels of shame—like a low-grade fever—making life manageable but mediocre. Such persons may be very successful but have no deep peace or consistent joy. Others have so much shame that life and relationships produce constant pain. For some, like Grace, shame becomes nearly fatal.

Why is there so much shame in the world?

Because shame works. It'll make you work like a dog. In fact, come to the dog track with me for an illustration.

the unreachable rabbit

The sport of dog racing can be tracked back as far as ancient Greece.

The modern version, however, found its genesis in (of all places) Arizona. On a horse track in Tucson, back in 1919, Oliver Smith had perfected a realistic mechanical rabbit for dogs to chase. Have you ever seen them race? The thoroughbred canines are poised behind their gates, clad in colorful numbered coats. The number tells the bettors, who cheer (or bite their nails depending on how much money they have wagered) their dog's position in the contest.

As the mechanically-propelled rabbit sprints in front of the dogs, the gates open and the greyhounds blast out of their confinement at full throttle. Lightning-fast, the dogs possess an amazing singleness of focus. *Get that thing! Get that rabbit. Get it! Bite it! Be there first!*

Somebody's dog wins. Somebody's loses. Some fans take home cash. Some leave broke. One dog might get a treat from his owner. Another might get a trophy for his dog house.

But no dog gets the rabbit.

Greyhounds may be one of the fastest animals in the world, but their brains must not be as fast as their legs. Wouldn't you think that after sprinting around a big track in an attempt to get a rabbit that no dog actually ever gets, you might reconsider next time? It seems like you would say to yourself, *Oh no, not the bunny thing again. I'm not going to run my legs off chasing an unreachable rabbit.* It seems like you would say, *Let 'em bet on somebody else, I'm going to spend my energy pursuing something I can really sink my teeth into.*

But the gullible dogs line up again in their gates the next day, certain that this time they'll finally catch the robot rabbit.

If I were Dr. Doolittle, I'd have a little counseling session with those sleek, handsome greyhounds. I'd inform them that the rabbit is a ruse. A trick. It's just a dream dangled in front of their sensitive noses for the express purpose of making them run like the wind. I'd have to break the news to them that even if they did the impossible and caught the rabbit, it would not satisfy their hunger. I'd have to let those dogs know that they were running their hearts out chasing a phony rabbit. A counterfeit bunny. A mirage. A futile goal.

If I could have a few unhurried moments with those greyhounds, I'd have to ask them a few questions: "How can you ever rest when the reward you're chasing is always moved just a little further in front of you? How can you ever have an authentic celebration if you can never catch the dream ahead? What does it feel like to pour every ounce of adrenaline, every sinew, every heartbeat into a pursuit that is destined to fail?"

I guess those dogs will keep chasing mechanical rabbits as long as they think the rabbit can be caught. But what happens if one day the dog admits to himself that he'll never be able to catch the hare? What happens if it suddenly dawns on the racing greyhound that he'll never quite make it? How could a dog live with himself if he finally admits that, no matter how fast he runs, he'll never be fast enough? How could you handle it if you realized that no matter how good you became, you'd never be good enough?

Wouldn't hope disappear? Wouldn't anxiety grow? Wouldn't you have to do something to stem the emotional anguish?

That's what happened to Grace McCracken. She had made an oath she couldn't possibly keep. She had devoted her life to earning what could never be earned.

Grace was the greyhound running hard after the rabbit she would never taste. Not in a lifetime. Though I've never been as depressed as Grace was, I can understand how tired she must have been. After all, I've run like a dog, too.

a rabbit called acceptance

I've run after the rabbit of acceptance. Oh, how I wanted to catch that thing! And how I've chased it through the years! With every fiber of my being. I suppose I could have spent my whole life leaping after it until I collapsed, spent and unfulfilled. Who knows what I might have sacrificed on the way. Health?

Marriage? Children? Peace? Joy? Calling?

People everywhere, all over the world, chase elusive rabbits. Maybe you're one of them. What does your rabbit look like?

We run harder when we are shamed because we are utterly desperate for love. From the first shock of cold air in the delivery room to the last gasp of air on our deathbeds, we crave love. We instinctively yearn for it, gravitate toward it, and feel like starving people if we're deprived of it. Our need for unfettered, unconditional, lavish love is so massive we'll do almost anything to get it. The drive to attain love (and its benefits of acceptance and significance) is so great in us that we'll devote everything we have to lay hold of it.

Take an honest self-inventory of what kind of family you grew up in and how you think and talk about yourself today. If you check any of the following boxes, you have shame issues that need healing.

The Way Shame-Based Families Think and Talk[2]

your family's statement *(beliefs and "rules" in your family)*	your own self-talk *(what you believe about yourself that was learned from your family)*
❏ **1 Performance over person** "How well you do determines who you are"	❏ **1 Human doing vs. human being** "My worth depends upon my ability to always do well"
❏ **2 Not allowed to make mistakes** "Stay within the lines; don't stumble; don't let others do better than you"	❏ **2 Perfectionism** "If I blow it, people will not accept me, appreciate me, or love me"
❏ **3 Cannot do it well enough** "You always do that wrong; you never get it just right; you could have done a better job"	❏ **3 Success sabotaging** "Things never work out for me; someone else could probably do a better job than me; that position is too important for me to accept"
❏ **4 Must always do better** "Never give full credit because they will stop trying"	❏ **4 Overachieving** "Have I done enough? Never mind the awards I've won, look what I haven't won yet"
❏ **5 Conditional support** "If you do things right, I'll support you; if you perform well enough, I'll really be proud of you"	❏ **5 Self-worth contingent on others** "I am okay only if you approve of me; what do you think of me? Do you think I did well enough?"
❏ **6 Undiscussed issues, secrets** "We're supposed to be a happy family, we don't talk about things like that." "It is in the past, so there is no need to talk about it; if you tell anyone, things will get worse for you"	❏ **6 Fear of discovery** "If people really knew about me, they would leave me. If people found out, they would think less of me"

If you're not aware of just how far you'll go to get love, you can be sure of this: Somebody else is. Chances are that someone has discovered he or she can get you to run if the rabbit called Love is dangled in front of your panting soul. This particular rabbit comes in a variety of shapes and sizes—approval, acceptance, affirmation, affection. Whatever you'll run after. And if you're like most, someone found out that the easiest way to get you to run harder and be better and do more is to dangle that love in front of you…just out of reach. But no matter how hard you tried—no matter how good a little boy or girl you were, the affirmation you wanted so deeply was never fully given.

It was withheld. So you would keep running.

And you did.

It might have been withheld because they were empty—the ones you wanted love from just didn't have it to give. It might have been withheld because they wanted you to do well and saw how fast and far you could run when love was withheld. It might have been withheld because of their ignorance. They thought, *We'd better not praise him too much. It might go to his head.* It might have been withheld because their energy was consumed by their addictions, and there was nothing left to show you real love. It might have been withheld because it was the only way they knew—they had run after rabbits all their lives, so it was your turn to learn to run.

For whatever reasons, people everywhere have tried and tried and tried to catch up to love. But despite their heroic efforts, millions have never tasted the real thing. Plainly put, shame is the painful feeling that there is some flaw in you that keeps you from catching the rabbit. So you just try harder and harder.

We all want people under our influence to be excellent and to accomplish great things. Parents want their children to behave. Teachers want their students to excel. Pastors want their parishioners to act like good Christians. That's why parents and teachers and pastors have championed the refrain: "*Shame on you.*" That's why we live in an atmosphere of shame. It's everywhere because it works...on the surface.

Shame can get kids to quit misbehaving.

Shame can compel students to make straight A's.

Shame can motivate parishioners to give more money.

People use shame to motivate others because they don't know the way of God. God never uses shame to motivate us toward right living or excellence. He never motivates us by withholding His love from us.

God does not motivate by withholding love, but by *giving* love.

One of my favorite Scripture verses occurs in the opening chapter of the Bible: "God blessed them and said to them, 'Be fruitful and increase in number; fill the earth and subdue it'" (Genesis 1:28).

Does God want us to be fruitful? Absolutely. Does God expect big things from us? He sure does. Does God bless people because they are fruitful? Nope.

Look again at the sequence in Genesis 1:28. The sequence is everything: God blessed Adam and Eve and *then* told them to be fruitful. The blessing came first. The affirmation of their worth did not rest upon their fruitfulness. Instead, their fruitfulness depended upon them knowing their self worth. The knowledge of their blessedness fueled their capacity to subdue the earth.

Most people imagine the message of Christianity runs something like this: *Love the Lord, do good, give generously, live right, serve God, and the Lord will really love you and bless you.*

That is not the Christian gospel! The true gospel certainly contains those three elements, but in different sequence. Here's the biblical formula: *God really loves you and has blessed you; therefore, love the Lord, do good, give generously, live right, and serve God.*

Shame does change behaviors—but it doesn't change hearts. In our efforts to control others, our shame seems to improve their outward lives, but inwardly, it sabotages their souls.

GRACE FINDS GRACE

By the spring of the year 2000, Grace McCracken had begun to give serious consideration to suicide. From the outside, you might not have seen it. After all, she had a nice house and a caring husband. But Grace's private world was wracked with pain—physically, mentally, and spiritually. She was too nervous to drive a car and often paralyzed emotionally by panic attacks. Medication didn't heal it. Psychotherapy didn't relieve it. Sleeping pills at night and stimulants in the morning couldn't touch it. Hiding in her house didn't restore it.

Grace McCracken had no friends, no hope, and no relief for her pain.

Secretly, however, people were praying for her. Grace's name foretold her story. Grace means God loved you before you loved Him.

As it turns out, some of our church members had made it their habit to prayer-walk their neighborhood. Almost every day, Mickey and Treva Thigpen and their daughter Olivia would pray as they walked past the McCracken home: "Lord, bless the people who live there and please give us a chance to show them the love of Jesus." That intercession is the only way I can explain how Grace one day found the courage to try church.

She had run out of doctors and had grown desperate. Church was the only thing she hadn't tried. So there she was on a Wednesday night. A bruised reed sitting in a class called Alpha for new Christians and seekers at our church. I was just walking through the room, meeting strangers who had come with a friend or who had responded to our newspaper ad, when I met Grace, her trembling hand in mine.

By her own later testimony, she was frightened by the mere interaction with people. I don't remember her looking me in the eye. She seemed ashamed to be there—in fact, feeling unworthy even to occupy the space.

She still can't tell you where or how she found the courage to come to church the following Sunday morning. She openly wept as the worship enveloped her and God-appointed worshipers smiled at her and spoke to her. Sometimes we weep just at the thought that real love might actually exist. Just a taste of the real thing and we will climb Mt. Everest to taste it again.

The following Wednesday night Grace returned to class and heard the video taped speaker say: "The gospel is like this: God has written you a check. It's yours free and clear. But you must accept, endorse, and deposit it in order to make use of it."

Grace sat at the table that night across from ministry leader

Bruce Lantelme and spoke four words that changed her life for-ever.

"I want that check."

It was like saying, *I want to live*. Grace met the only Person in the world who truly has life to give. Grace met the source of all grace, Jesus Christ.

In that redemptive encounter, God had made Grace's spirit alive. Next, the Lord began healing her soul. Grace can't find words to explain what happened the next Sunday morning after the church service. She says that she walked with an unknown courage to the prayer room where three lay counselors placed hands on her and began to pray. What followed was a two hour bath in the loving presence of the Holy Spirit. The prison door to her cell of shame opened that day and she stepped out.

When I saw Grace one week later, I couldn't believe it! The bruised reed was standing tall like an oak. The quivering hand and voice were replaced by the jitters of real joy. Mourning had become dancing. In fact, she was downright giddy. Everything became new.

Her husband later told me that Grace noticed the sea shells on the beaches as if she'd never seen them. She saw stars shimmering in the heavens where, before, she had seen only a dark canopy. And she saw people—real friends, scores of them, flooding into her life. Grace now leads our follow-up ministry for new believers and seekers. If you met her today, you would be overwhelmed by her contagious joy and quiet confidence. In fact, after meeting her, you'd question whether I had exaggerated the depth of her former depression. And I'd tell you that I hadn't revealed the half of it.

When Grace encountered the expansive, unmerited

affection of the Messiah, she found herself approved, not because she had performed well, but because Jesus had. It was a gigantic reversal of what she always had believed since girlhood. She thought love was a reward for good behavior. She assumed that perfect love was therefore reserved only for perfect people. All she had known to do was to try harder.

But Grace didn't need to try harder.

Neither do you.

Pause for a moment. Breathe it in deeply as I tell you again:

You don't need to try harder. You are already loved.

Grace, like you and I, only needed to lift her eyes, look into the face of the Savior, behold His smile, feel His affection, accept His provision, and know herself to be a creature of infinite worth. She had to take the hand of Christ, be ushered into her heavenly Father's intimate presence, and hear the God of the universe declare: "This is My daughter, in whom I'm well pleased." Only then, when her shame was lifted, did the anxiety evaporate like a mist under the rising sun. Only then, were the roots of depression plucked from her soul.

Grace's name had prophesied her destiny. Only grace could have healed Grace. Only grace could have healed me. Only grace can heal you.

DOMINOES OF GRACE

You've heard of a living Nativity at Christmas time? On Easter Day 2002, I announced a "Living New Testament"; a living book of Acts. It's how the gospel was always meant to be shared. One after the other, people came forward to tell their story.

First, I introduced the Thigpens who had prayed for Grace before knowing her. Then Grace came forward, retelling the story of her healing and transformation. Next, I told of Bob Hall, Grace's neighbor who recommitted his life to the Lord after Grace and Treva Thigpen started praying for him. Then Bobby's brother and sister-in-law, Gerry and Doris Hall, came forward. At their back yard pool, Gerry and Doris hosted a baptismal service for what seemed like half their neighborhood and made renewed commitments to serving Christ themselves.

Next came Kim Kale. Doris Hall had given her a tape of Grace's testimony. Kim was so touched that she opened her heart and became a born-again disciple of Jesus Christ, too. Phyllis Taylor came forward next. She wasn't a neighbor of Grace's but she found out through Doris about the back yard baptisms, had made a decision for Christ, and had come to be baptized for the first time. Finally, Grace's husband, Denny McCracken, stepped forward. Grace had led him to Christ some months earlier. He was immersed in that pool, too.

"What led you to accept Christ as your Savior, Denny?" I asked in front of the church.

"I was given back the wife I married thirty years ago."

As I listened to all these beautiful people share how Christ had touched them, I thought back to the trembling leaf of a hand I had felt in mine when Grace was still under shame. I realized then that not only had the bruised reed grown into a blossoming tree, but behold, sweet fruit was dropping from her branches.

How ironic. As long as Grace was striving to be strong and

ASK   A Question to Inquire:

What "rabbits" have I chased and why?

BELIEVE   A Principle to Ponder:

"The sequence is everything: God blessed Adam and Eve and *then* told them to be fruitful. The blessing came first."

I do not have to be fruitful in order to be blessed. I am blessed and, therefore, I can be fruitful.

CHOOSE   A Commitment to Keep:

I choose today to quit pursuing that which cannot be caught. I will no longer seek to earn love because love cannot be earned. I will surrender my efforts to prove myself acceptable.

pray

O God, You have promised that I have been blessed with every spiritual blessing in Christ and that I have been qualified through Christ for my inheritance among the saints. I'm so tired of running. Be my Sabbath rest. Allow me to know the sweetness of Your acceptance. Show me the way off my racetrack and onto Your path of abundant life. Today, I relinquish my futile efforts to find self-worth through performance, and I invite Your Holy Spirit to flood my heart with the assurance that I am Your beloved child. In Jesus' name, AMEN.

CHAPTER THREE

a rose for a rose

When our church hosted a large denominational gathering, we adorned the meeting rooms with dozens of roses. Appreciating the beauty of the roses, I had a sudden inspiration: *On Valentine's weekend, we'll honor each woman in church with the gift of a rose.*

It seemed like a homerun idea. (How could it lose?) If nothing else, I figured it would be a simple, memorable token of affection in honor of all the women.

I could never have imagined what it became instead.

What happened on that unforgettable Sunday melted our hearts, and demonstrated the incomparable power of honesty, love, and honor to heal shame.

On Friday morning, as I began preparing and praying for my Sunday message, my thoughts turned to the women dearest to me.

I thought of my mother, a woman familiar with heartache, and whose faith was born in the adversity of a broken marriage. I thought of her tender love, her tenacity of spirit. I recalled her testimony of the day she cried out to heaven, "O Lord, if You are there, I need You to do something. I'm sinking down, and Lord, if You don't do something, I'll probably take these three boys down with me."

Soon after that desperate cry, my mother's friend knocked on the door. She explained that she had been awakened in the night with an overwhelming desire to pray for Mom. I remembered it all again. It's how a mother and her three boys met Jesus.

I thought of my own wife of nearly twenty years. I marveled again at the magnificence of her character, her joy for living, and her perseverance through tragedy. I knew I had never betrayed her, would never leave her, and would always love her. But that Friday morning, my spirit became acutely sensitive, and I felt the pain of a woman's soul whose husband's attention was too often distracted by the demands of ministry.

Turning aside from my computer and commentaries, in the quietness of my little study, I openly repented of any way that I had ever dishonored my wife.

What began as a moment of personal confession grew into...something else—a transforming encounter with God. A Holy Presence suddenly captured my heart, and (difficult as it is to explain) I began to feel the weight of shame and dishonor that men have shown women for generations. I cannot describe the holiness of those hours I experienced with God. If we are ever given even the smallest glimpse of the consequences of shame in our world, believe me, it's too much for us.

a CONFESSION

My tears that day became a private stream of grief on behalf of women. I realized that the conviction I was experiencing was not merely for my own sin, but for the sin of men everywhere. I knew it was biblical to confess on behalf of others. Nehemiah did so and God heard his prayer. But that Friday morning, God Himself put a spirit of confession in me. It was full of love and void of condemnation—but God utterly broke my heart over our society's dishonor of women.

For the next hour, I wept and wrote my confession to women everywhere. I knew I would share it Sunday morning. And I knew I would never look on a woman the same again.

I had told only a handful of people my plans for Sunday morning. We had ordered the roses weeks earlier. I wish you could have seen the look on the face of the store clerk when we picked up 360 individual red roses on that Saturday! When I told her we were giving a rose to every woman at church the next morning, she gasped out loud: "What church is that?!" I told her, smiled, and thought again, *When will we learn that honor preaches better than shame?*

It seemed important to me that only men prepare the roses. So while I met with prayer partners before the service, several men clumsily wrapped each long-stemmed rose in green waxed paper. I don't think we did it properly or with much class, but as one woman commented later, "It wouldn't have mattered to us if they had been wrapped in wadded newspaper." Meanwhile, as I prayed with intercessors, I wept inexplicable tears.

I managed to preach a brief message from the Genesis account of the Fall. Adam, before their sin, treasured Eve. "This is now bone of my bones and flesh of my flesh." I identified the essence of Paradise, "they were not ashamed." I pointed out how, in the midst of Eve's temptation, Adam was silent. He was there, but he did not defend the woman.[3]

Created to be spiritual warriors, we men were designed to be the first to our knees, the first to the cross, the first to wield the sword of the Word. But in the heat of the battle, Adam suddenly went passive. Winston Churchill was right when he said that all it takes for a society to fall is for "good men to do nothing."

I called attention to Adam's demeanor after the Fall. He was ashamed. Afraid. So he hid. And when God asked, "Who told you that you were naked? Have you eaten from the tree…?" Adam tried to shift the blame: "The woman you put here with me—she gave me some fruit from the tree, and I ate it." Rather than confessing, repenting, and releasing his shame to his Maker, the man attempted to shame the woman instead. She was the closest scapegoat, and he used her to feel momentarily better about himself.

It's a pattern that has been repeated through the millennia. From the earliest instance of sin, we men have tended toward passivity in the midst of spiritual battle and then, in the wake of our failures, blamed women to soften our anxiety and shame.

It was all I could do to utter those succinct interpretations of Scripture. I could no longer fight back my emotion. Stepping to the floor level amongst the people, I told the church what had happened to me on Friday morning and began to confess to women on behalf of men. I spoke as if I had personally committed the sins. The women in church that day heard a sovereign God capture a young preacher's voice for His mysterious purposes.

It was neither emotionalism nor theater. There was no rational explanation. But my confession began to pour out:

I have glimpsed the pain of the dishonored and shamed women in our world.... I believe God has sent me to you today to say I am sorry for not honoring you.

I'm sorry for the way that men have abandoned women. To every little girl, whose daddy was too busy at work to notice her playschool art...for every dance recital that we missed because of needing to work late one more night...for every preacher's daughter whose father was out saving the world but didn't notice he was losing his own girl...I'm truly sorry.

When the moment of battle rises, and the dragon rears its ugly head, we were meant to fight—to do something, even if it's the wrong thing. But we have been too silent, too passive, and we have left you to fight your own battle.

We've left our adolescent girls to find out about their sexuality in the backseat of the boy's car, rather than in the open conversation and sanctity of our home. I am sorry for our silence—that we haven't spoken to you more. And I'm sorry that we have been so unable to show our daughters affection. You wanted to roll in the grass, to ride on our shoulders, to feel the whiskers on our cheeks, and to sit in our laps for long stretches of time. But we've been uncomfortable with touch because we weren't taught it by our fathers....

I want to say I'm sorry for every little girl and every wife whose daddy or husband abandoned her for a bottle of alcohol. When you needed us, we just weren't there.

I want to say that I'm sorry for every little girl or wife whose daddy or husband left home and didn't come back. You were the hidden treasure and we didn't know it. We thought we could find it at the end of the rainbow, over some distant horizon...but the rainbow had no end, and there was no other treasure, and for too many of us, it's now too late.

I'm sorry for the ways we have used you for our advantage. No, I am not the child molester, nor the rapist, nor the man sitting at the bar watching you dance around a pole, nor the John who was your last customer. I have not, by the grace of God been that man. But what man in our midst has not sinned by looking upon a woman as an object rather than a person, putting expectations upon your waistline that we do not put upon our own. We have bought the cars and the calendars that the bikini models modeled. I feel the whole weight of the unthinkable ways that we have used women to momentarily soothe our deep inward shame.

...May I tell you—if we could be honest with ourselves, with God, and with you—how most men really feel? We marvel at who you are. You have discernment that we don't have. You notice tiny, subtle details when we see nothing at all. We marvel at the way you make relationships, and we secretly long to be able to find friends the way you do. We're amazed at the way you pray, the way you sing, the way you smile, the way you laugh, the way you cry. We're amazed at how deeply you feel things and how easily you express those feelings. We are amazed at how multidimensional you are—interweaving softness and strength; how you have endured so much, persevered through so much, and celebrated so much.

Every woman is a rose. Lovely, mysterious, fragrant, and meant to be handled with care. Its piercing thorns greet only those who recklessly grab the stem without taking time to appreciate its total beauty. The most beautiful of flowers, the sweetest of fragrances, and the costliest in the florist's shop. You are beautiful from the moment of the first bud, but your beauty unfolds a petal at a time as you blossom and grow. Today, we honor you. We do not seek to own you, use you, sell you, or control you—but to admire you. And thank you.

Without fanfare or manipulation I then announced to the men that I was going to kneel at the front of the church and tell God how sorry I was and ask His help to be a different, better man, and that any man was welcome to come join me. Almost every man in the church rushed forward, buried his face in the carpet, and repented with me. As I closed those moments of deep repentance, we brought out a table displaying hundreds of red roses.

"Men," I said with a smile, "we have come here today not only to repent of dishonoring and shifting our shame to women, but we have come to honor them. Would you help me give a gift to every woman here—married and single, young and old? And as you give a rose to a woman tell her, 'A *rose for a rose.*'"

Heaven must be like the scene I beheld—an atmosphere void of shame and full of honor. Imagine hundreds of men making their way up and down the aisles, in and out of pews, whispering, "A rose for a rose." As the aroma of roses filled our sanctuary, so did the aroma of Christ. The fragrance of sweet grace intoxicated us, and our hearts were laid open to the cleansing mercy of God.

I had not orchestrated it. I was not analyzing it. Only later did I realize that we had just dealt a mortal blow to the spirit of shame. For those moments, we men moved opposite to shame. Instead of hiding, we came forward, humbled ourselves publicly, and called to God for help. For once, instead of silently fearing the exposure of our faults, we admitted our inadequacy to God and to the women we sought to honor. For once, we were unconcerned about our performance because we felt the power of God surging through our hearts.

In the words of Gordon Dalbey, we had decided to fight like men—from our knees. With a gift of honor, we fought back the power of the Enemy. As we wept, confessed, and whispered our honor to women, we knew that we were, at least for that morning, real men.

I had not imagined the transformation it would make in me

or in our men. And I had not begun to fathom the healing it would bring to women. We received unprecedented numbers of audio-tape requests. Word spread across our city. Manuscripts of the confession were multiplied hundreds of times.

I don't remember ever receiving so many letters telling of God's healing work. I was most moved by the words from a woman I'll call Cindy.

Dear Pastor Alan,

The effect this morning's service had on me has left me with a compelling need to let you know. You see, I have suffered dishonor at the hands of men in my life, but the one that has bruised my petals the most is my relationship with my father. I am the preacher's daughter you spoke to this morning.... The extreme legalism we practiced in our family caused me to grow up ostracized and lonely. I married young to escape and found myself in an abusive relationship.... Many years later, my husband abandoned our three girls and me.... I had made no effort to reconcile. One day, sitting at my kitchen table, my father quietly berated my "unforgiving heart".... Several years later...my father refused to share in my joy or rejoice that I had found [a new husband] who honored me and treated me with respect and dignity. He refused to attend our wedding or even acknowledge our marriage.

This morning, at first I felt a weight of hurt and grief as I wept when you voiced the apology to the preacher's daughter. But as the service progressed and I witnessed the conviction of the Spirit on a whole congregation of men and continued to hear your words of blessing, I was overwhelmed with a feeling of cleansing and healing like I have never experienced. It was as if my father himself had made things right. A heavy weight has been lifted from my heart and the chains of hurt were shattered.... My bruised petals are healed and my joy could fill a rose garden!

IN agreement with your pain

God knows your needs. He is a Great High Priest who sympathizes with every emotional wound. If I, an earthly, sinful man, can have my own heart broken by a small glimpse of the wounds of our shame, what must the unblemished God, whose whole nature is love, feel for His children?

Chances are, the people who have hurt you, dishonored you, or abandoned you will never recognize the depth of their errors nor the depth of your pain. For all who will never receive a confession from those who have hurt them, would you allow me to say "I'm sorry"?

Confession simply means "agreeing with." If I confess to you on behalf of those who've harmed you, I am not presuming to undo their offense; I am merely agreeing with God's own heart that you have suffered what you were never meant to suffer. Make sure you have a moment of uninterrupted quiet. God wants to touch your heart.

On behalf of the silent others, I confess…

...To every child who spilled her milk on Mommy's clean floor, or whose legs were too little to keep up with Daddy, or whose ordinary childish acts of irresponsibility were met with shame instead of understanding, I'm truly sorry. Please forgive us. We parents often treat our children as if they are already adults. You were just acting the way a little child acts. You didn't have the dexterity to never spill your milk. You didn't have the leg span to always keep up. We reprimanded you for breaking rules that you didn't even know were rules, and we acted disgusted with you for not understanding what no one had ever taught you. Forgive us.

...To every school child who was teased on the school bus, or the playground, or laughed at in the classroom, I confess. The saying should be reversed: "Sticks and stones can break my bones, but your words can really hurt me." For every nickname, every taunt, and every smirk from every bully or brat, I'm sorry. We didn't realize we were eroding your soul. We secretly felt so bad about ourselves that we had to put others down in order to feel worthwhile. Forgive us.

...To every child of parents of who were too busy, I'm sorry. We were busy making money or making a name or building a business, and we didn't realize that we had sacrificed you on the way. Forgive us.

...To every child of parents who were too consumed with their hatred of one another to notice you, I'm sorry. While your parents fought, all you ever received was the table scraps of bitterness and the rinds of our rage. Forgive us.

…To every child who never knew a father, I'm sorry. I knew how to sleep with a woman but not how to marry her and nurture her. I knew how to make a baby but not how to father a child. I have no idea what I missed. Please forgive me.

…To every child whose father left, I'm sorry. I fooled myself into thinking I could leave your mother without it seeming like I was leaving you. I didn't know that you would lose sleep wondering what you did wrong. Please forgive me.

…To every child who was born a girl but whose parents wanted a boy, I'm so sorry. I didn't know that my little jokes were like daggers to your soul. God made you who you are because of His perfect plan. It wasn't you I was displeased with, it was really me. Oh, please forgive us. Be your beautiful self.

…To every child of an alcoholic, I'm sorry. I can't believe that I let a bottle capture my attention more than you. It was not my lack of love for you that led me to drink—it was a lack of love for myself. While I was anesthetizing my anxiety, you were being abandoned. Forgive me.

…To every school child who was shamed by a teacher. We wanted you to learn fast so that we would look like good teachers. We didn't have the patience to spend the time with you that you really needed. We didn't know that singling you out for scorn was cursing your life. Forgive us.

...To every child from a performance-based home. Success and looking good meant everything to us. When we pushed you to excel we didn't realize that you thought you were only valuable when you were succeeding. We're sorry for all the pressure we put on you. We hurried you up through childhood and put all our broken dreams onto you, for you to somehow magically fulfill. Forgive us.

...To every employee who was belittled or mistreated by a supervisor, I'm sorry. The workplace was the place I shifted my shame. You had to take it, your job depended on it. I never stopped to think about your sleepless nights and gnawing anxiety that were the product of my pride. Forgive me.

...To every church member who ever left church feeling worse than before. We thought that we were being bold and "really preaching the gospel" when we shamed you over and over. But we weren't. It wasn't the gospel at all. God wanted you convicted, so you could be filled with the hope of change. We condemned you and left you with no instruction on how to change. You needed an encounter with the most winsome Person in the universe, Jesus Christ, and we gave you a set of rules. The rules were good, but they were impossible to keep without the power of the Holy Spirit. Forgive us.

...To every victim of incest, rape, and abuse. My soul was diseased. I was famished for approval. I abused you as the ultimate shifting of my shame. You did not invite it, nor deserve it. The horror of my deeds demonstrates not the depth of a flaw in you, but the depth of disgust I had for myself. I left you to bear the weight of the shame because I didn't know how to give it to Jesus. Forgive me.

breaking free

The cycle of shame can only be broken when repentance replaces bitterness. Shame can only be healed when honor replaces dishonor. To let go of shame, you must let go of your sinful reaction to it. Be angry, but do not sin. Hold no judgment. Harbor no resentment. Nourish no bitter root. Whether your repentance is primarily for the shame you've inflicted or the unforgiveness you've harbored, now is the time to change. I can confess sins on the behalf of others, but no one can repent for you.

Repent. Then turn your eyes heavenward to the Source of grace and honor. As the psalmist declared, "The LORD God is a sun and shield; the LORD bestows favor and honor" (Psalm 84:11).

Eons ago, seeing the devastating consequences of the shame that slithered into the Garden and into the fabric of humanity, Father God knew that healing would require an expensive gift of honor. He saw the shame of His betrothed, and instead of sending her more condemnation, He sent His most fragrant offering. He sent the beauty of His holiness. The thorns upon the Savior's brow would only accentuate the aroma of His grace. God sent a rose to His beloved—He sent the Rose of Sharon.

Behold Christ's beauty.

Breathe in the fragrance of His mercy.

It is God's highest act of honor to His people—a Rose for a rose.

ASK   A Question to Inquire:

What bitter roots have sprung in my heart from the seeds of shame?

BELIEVE   A Principle to Ponder:

"The cycle of shame only can be broken when repentance replaces bitterness. Shame only can be healed when honor replaces dishonor."

No matter what depths of shame I've experienced, I need harbor no bitterness, judgment, or resentment. I can be angry, but not sin. I can grieve, but have hope.

CHOOSE   A Commitment to Keep:

I choose today to release bitterness, judgment, and resentment from my heart. While I may not have received an apology from my offenders, I forgive them on the confession of another. While I do not excuse the offense, I lift the offender unto God for His blessing.

pRay

O God, You have promised to never leave me
nor forsake me. You have always been there—even when
I've been most ashamed. Heal my deepest wounds.
I worship You in the beauty of Your holiness and open my
heart to receive the honor You have shown me in the gift of
Jesus Christ. I receive the fragrant offering of the Rose of
Sharon. Let me breathe in the aroma of Your mercy and
behold Your beauty. Fill me with the supernatural grace to
let go of all roots of bitterness. I release
(name those who've shamed you) to You, choosing to
hold no resentment against my offender and asking You
to bless him/her instead. As You have forgiven me,
I forgive others. In Jesus' name, AMEN.

CHAPTER FOUR

the sting of a hidden hornet

I t was the first year in my first church, with 117 people on the roll.

Fresh out of seminary, I planned to be Super-Pastor to each and every one. I would respond to crises in parishioners' lives faster than a speeding bullet. I would leap tall buildings to rescue one lone sheep. And with my x-ray vision, I would see into the secret needs of every member and solve all their problems. One late summer day in Durham, North Carolina, Super-Pastor had a chance to strut his stuff.

I knew this man (I'll call him Ralph) would be a challenge. He was one of those jokesters with a rough edge who you know has a big heart—if you could ever get to it through that thick hide surrounding it. We're talking alligator-skin thick. Tortoise-shell thick.

But I was Super-Pastor, liked the challenge, and loved Ralph.

That's why I made sure I showed up at his brother's funeral.

It would be an opportunity for him to release his grief—and an opportunity for me to unleash my newly-mined pastoral prowess.

My wife and I waited for the crowd to begin disbursing after the minister finished the graveside benediction. We drifted over toward Ralph and his wife, passing under the shade of a great oak tree.

Then came our moment.

Our sublime, ridiculous moment.

You must envision the scene rightly in order to get the impact of the unforgettable episode. Four of us were under the tree—Ralph and his wife, me and my wife. As I began to speak, all eyes turned toward me.

"Ralph," I uttered softly in my Super-Pastor tones, "this must be a difficult time for you."

"Yeah, I guess so," Ralph said in his usual terse way.

Then, the moment. Ralph's voice cracked: "Yeah, it's tough, pastor. That was the last of my brothers…only me left now."

As I reached my arm behind me to pat myself on the back for being the Super-Pastor who could get even the calloused Ralph to share his burden, I couldn't believe my eyes.

My wife—my dear, beautiful wife who always wanted to be a pastor's wife and who was willing to come out on a hot afternoon to a nonmember funeral—began to display a peculiar countenance. Out of necessity, I let go of my Super-Pastor listening posture long enough to glance at her face. She is a very expressive woman, to say the least, but this was an expression I had not seen before.

She winced with pained impatience.

I shot a glance back at her with a flash of disbelief, communicating my message with only my eyes: *I don't know what in the world is wrong with you—but get a grip. This is an important, pastoral moment. I am, after all, Super-Pastor.*

She saw my look. She knew what it meant. But the grimace on her face grew worse. Then, to my horror, she began crouching over at the hips. She bent one leg inward toward the other like a three-year old in need of the potty. I considered the open grave and weighed the benefit of leaping in it as a suitable escape from the inevitable humiliation heading my way.

Ralph, as yet, hadn't noticed. He continued to open his long-shuttered heart, eyes moistening with tears (perhaps for the first time in his whole calloused life). I let my glance meet Anne's again. If you ask me, I'd say my eyes portrayed a serious look—as she tells it, "daggers." But despite my steely stare, she crouched over even further.

And then, surely for the first time in the history of Christianity—a pastor's wife, standing under an oak tree by a grave, listening to a grieving parishioner, hiked up her dress into a ball around her midriff.

We all stared in awe.

Suddenly she exclaimed, "Something's *biting* me! I've got to get to the car!"

After muttering a quick apology to Ralph and his wife, we made the journey to our car, which, having been at the rear of the funeral procession, was located in a different zip code from the oak tree. What a spectacle—Anne clutching her dress in a ball, walking with a crouching limp and repeating, "Something is biting the fire out of me…biting the fire out of me…biting the fire out of me…."

As we closed in on our car, I could only think about the sudden need to update my résumé. And even if I somehow held onto my job, how could I ever face Ralph again? I murmured below my breath, "This better not be a gnat bite."

Once at the car, my normally modest wife hoisted her dress up even higher and clutched a huge ball of garment with both fists. "It's in there!" she yelled, pointing at the clump of fabric she was grasping. "I'm going to fling it out—you do something when it comes out, Alan!"

To my surprise and her redemption, out flew a big, angry hornet.

After some time had passed and I gained a more charitable perspective, I knew my wife had wanted to support her Super-Pastor husband, and had no desire at all to disrespect Ralph. But when that hornet stung her, it wouldn't have mattered if Anne had been talking to the Queen of England. She had to let her pain be known—and she had to get the culprit out. And Super-Pastor had to fall from his pedestal.

As soon as you stop laughing at us, think about this question: What's stinging you that you're too ashamed to uncover?

You might not have a hornet in your dress, but I've never met anyone who had no inner pain. What's your hidden hornet? Deep loneliness? Unhealed emotional wounds? Repeated rejections? An alcoholic dad?

Think about Anne's predicament under the old oak tree and you'll get a glimpse of the deeper problem of shame. Anne was getting stung, literally. She felt the pain, but she also felt trapped in two ways. First, a proper pastor's wife doesn't just suddenly hike up her dress in the midst of mourners at a graveside.

Second, she saw the scorn in my Super-Pastor eyes. Put those two together and you have a tough dilemma—endure the pain of a stinging hornet or endure the shame.

Only when the pain of the sting gets worse than the pain of the shame do people become willing to let their agony be known.

Why do we do that? Why do we hide the pain of our shame rather than facing it? The answer is as ancient as humanity itself.

paradise Lost

God gave Adam and Eve a luxurious, sumptuous garden in which to live, eat, work, and play. Literal paradise. The very thing we all long to experience. There was limitless provision, unhindered learning, and a strong sense of vocation and purpose. There was no disease, no death, no despair. No worry, no hurry, no fury. But it wasn't the absence of famine or even the absence of funeral homes that made Eden a paradise.

It was the total absence of shame.

There was no such thing as shame before sin entered the world. In fact, the only thing that God deemed important enough to record in the Bible about Adam and Eve's relationship before the Fall was that "the man and his wife were both naked, and they felt no shame" (Genesis 2:25).

Scripture allows us no glimpse of their pre-Fall conversations. We have no idea what they looked like or what they liked to do with their unlimited time. We don't know if they liked to ride horses or hold hands or smell the flowers. All we need to know about the character of a sinless relationship can be summarized in that one phrase: "they felt no shame."

We can't even imagine how delicious that feeling must be. If you can remember doing something really great, in which you felt really proud of yourself and everyone else was congratulating you and admiring you, then you have the beginning of understanding it. You feel like you are on top of the world. You might have felt shame-free for an instant when you asked a girl to the prom for the first time and she said yes. Or when you received a letter of acceptance to the college you always wanted to attend. It's the bliss of total acceptance and self-worth.

Unfortunately, our shame-free feelings are fleeting. I felt shame free for a few hours after being married to the most wonderful woman in the world. After all, if she loved me enough to join me for life, I couldn't be that bad. And on a honeymoon no one expects anything of you except to enjoy your new mate. Even so, when we pulled into the fancy honeymoon hotel, I bumbled uncomfortably trying to tip the valet parking attendant, revealing my inexperience with such niceties.

The bellman grinned knowingly.

"Honeymooners?"

Suddenly I was ashamed that I was so youthful and had such little sophistication. If we're honest, even our most shame-free moments are quickly eclipsed by somebody's criticism or, more frequently, our self-criticism.

To say that Adam and Eve "felt no shame" means they never had a moment of wondering if the other was thinking something critical. It means they never had the slightest fear that if they said something silly or weren't romantic enough or bought the wrong birthday present that they would be rejected.

Eve never once worried that Adam would criticize her for eating one too many strawberries (was there chocolate in Paradise?) or that Adam would cast an eye toward a bikini clad coed on the beach.

For his part, Adam never once felt that gnawing fear that Eve would be disappointed in his career choice or that she would make him feel like a bad husband for showing up fifteen minutes late to dinner. In a shame-free relationship, every ounce of their energy went into exploring their future rather than covering their tracks.

A world with no shame is pure paradise. It's a picture of heaven.

The Lord made one—and only one—prohibition to the First Couple in Eden: "You are free to eat from any tree in the garden; but you must not eat from the tree of the knowledge of good and evil, for when you eat of it you will surely die" (Genesis 2:16–17). A seductive serpent slithered into their paradise and deceived them, saying, "You will not surely die." So Adam and Eve ate of the forbidden fruit. They broke God's law, broke God's heart, and broke their fellowship with God.

Notice the starkness of this contrast. The only thing we know about their relationship before their sin was that "they felt no shame." After they ate the forbidden fruit, the first thing we learn was that "the eyes of both of them were opened, and they realized they were naked; so they sewed fig leaves together and made coverings for themselves" (Genesis 3:7).

The primary pain that entered the world with sin was the anguish of shame. If you think of sin as the disease, shame is its primary symptom. Don't mistake the Genesis account as merely about the embarrassment of having uncovered genitalia. Outward exposure can feel embarrassing, but it's nothing like having your soul stripped bare.

the dynamics of shame

Imagine sitting in church and suddenly, during the sermon, a picture of you appears on the big projection screen and all of the thoughts you've had that week are exposed for the whole church to see. One embarrassing thought after another— moments of silent lust, jealous thoughts about other church members, critical thoughts toward the people on your pew. If you can imagine that horror, you're beginning to get the sense of sheer terror that Adam and Eve suddenly felt.

Now, to understand the power of this darkness, imagine being relegated to a life in which, everywhere you went, your failures, flaws, and ugly thoughts were posted constantly for all to see. If you can envision that, you can begin to understand the ultimate pain. If paradise can be defined as the place of no shame, then author Gordon Dalbey must be right: "Hell is...trying to bear your own shame."[4]

Suddenly the only people who ever experienced a sinless earth were thrust into the grip of shame. The pain of it was so great that Adam and Eve began to take immediate steps to relieve the feeling of shame. So their sin grew. And a terrible, downward cycle of destruction began.

We all do it to some degree. Our shame is so painful, and we have so much anxiety about our failures, that we'll do just about anything to cover it up. The shame just hurts so much that we anesthetize ourselves. We're trying to get back into paradise—the place of no shame.

- Liquor's intoxication makes the alcoholic momentarily unaware of his shame—but it doesn't put him back into Eden.
- The overeater momentarily masks the pain of shame with the pleasure of food—but it doesn't reproduce Paradise.
- The rebellious teenager avoids the pain by pretending he doesn't care.
- The perfectionist hides behind the satisfaction of accomplishment.

We use different shapes and sizes, but we all wear fig leaves of some sort.

Shame is insidious. It inflicts not only the pain of feeling really bad about ourselves, but then it begins a cycle that blocks us from taking the only steps that can help us feel better. As Adam and Eve began hiding from one another, they also began hiding from God. "Then the man and his wife heard the sound of the LORD God as he was walking in the garden in the cool of the day, and they hid from the LORD God among the trees of the garden" (Genesis 3:8).

HIDING AND SEEKING

One of Shame's greatest goals is to get you hiding from God. Why? Because His rewards go to seekers, not hiders. "God looks down from heaven on the sons of men to see if there are...any who seek God" (Psalm 53:2). We have a God who "rewards those who earnestly seek him" (Hebrews 11:6). Shame therefore steals not only the joy of knowing yourself to be infinitely valuable, but also steals all the blessings that come to those who seek God.

Shame's invitation is: "Hide from God lest you be condemned." Jesus' invitation is: "Seek first his kingdom and his righteousness, and all these things will be given to you as well" (Matthew 6:33).

Adam and Eve weren't only hiding from God and from each other, they were also hiding from themselves. That's really what Adam was doing when he tried shifting the blame toward Eve: *"The woman you put here with me...."*

The seventeenth-century Reformer John Calvin wrote two volumes of theology that helped shape the future of Christian thought. His *Institutes of the Christian Religion* begins with one of the most important statements of the entire work: "True religion consists of knowledge of God and knowledge of self."[5] God is not hiding from us. He *wants* to be known.

Shame, however, lures people into hiding from God. It keeps us from knowing God and knowing ourselves. Avoiding the pain involved in genuine self-inventory, we rationalize and shift blame. That's what Adam did. Instead of honestly facing his sin and quickly going to his Father for forgiveness, the weight of shame compelled Adam to deny his own heart problem. "If we claim to be without sin, we deceive ourselves.... If we confess our sins, he...will...purify us..." (1 John 1:8–9).

Shame begins with the tempter's deception, but is propelled by self-deception. The self-deceived life never benefits from God's purifying purposes. The only thing that can keep us from knowing God is our decision to hide from Him. The only thing that can keep us from the cleansing stream of God's mercy is our decision to hide from ourselves.

It sure doesn't help matters when our whole society seems to encourage us to hide from God, from others, and from ourselves. I think of all the parents who, upon losing their patience, tell their children abruptly: "Go to your room."

Why tell them that? The tone of the parent's voice says it: "I am so frustrated with you that I don't even want to see your face right now." The message is easily translated: "Go off by yourself and bear your own shame." So we are taught from our earliest days that the consequences of misbehavior are isolation and shame. We learn that our parents don't want to hear about our feelings of inward shame. We are encouraged to grab the closest fig leaves. And others will help us get suited up. It's tantamount to saying: "I don't care how bad the bee is stinging you, don't lift your dress up around me."

We were born in the spirit and shame of Adam. We do all that we possibly can to cover over our pain. And the hidden hornet keeps on stinging.

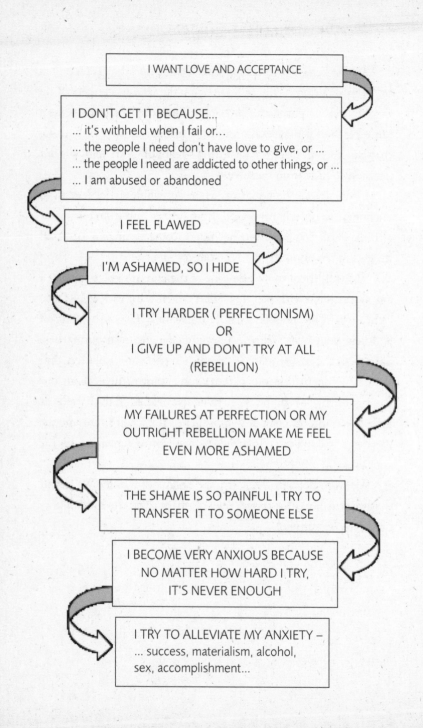

a new covering

What's the alternative to hiding? Crouching in a cemetery with your dress hiked up into a ball? I hope not! Can you just suddenly come out of hiding and stand naked and unashamed? No, you still need a covering.

Dudley Hall's words, in his shame-busting book *Grace Works*, tell it with a chuckle:

I was raised in the rural South. Many churches in the area where I grew up had baptismal pools concealed under the pulpit platform. When it was time for baptism, they simply moved the pulpit, opened up the floor, and poured in the water. Often they would hang curtains on each side of the front so the men and women could change clothes separately. One Sunday night, in one of these churches, a woman was being baptized. As she was lowered into the water, she slipped. She reached behind her to grab onto something solid. But what she grabbed, unfortunately, was the curtain surrounding the men's dressing room. The curtain fell. And there, in all his nakedness, stood the next baptismal candidate. Panicked, he clutched for something to hold in front of him. The nearest thing he could find was a straight-backed chair. So there he crouched, holding the chair in front of him, with this awful look of horror on his face. One of the deacons of the church, seeking to help the situation, ran to the back of the building and switched off the light. The nervous, rumbling giggle of the congregation went on as five interminable minutes passed. Finally, believing that the poor man had been given enough time to get dressed, the deacon switched on the light. And there, paralyzed by his fear, was the man—still crouched behind the chair. I suppose he just wasn't sure when the light would be turned back on![6]

If a chair is all you have to cover your nakedness, then a chair's your best friend! Shamed people dread the idea of being exposed because they think God will strip away their chair or fig leaf and leave them standing there even more ashamed. The fear of being stripped naked makes us hide all the more stubbornly.

Here's the good news. Even though Adam and Eve had broken God's only prohibition and had introduced sin into a sinless world, God didn't yank off their fig leaves.

Instead, He gave them a better set of clothes.

"The LORD God made garments of skin for Adam and his wife and clothed them" (Genesis 3:21). Please notice that the first covering for shame required shed blood. Fig leaves fade. Sacrificed animal skins last a while longer.

But God had a permanent covering in the making.

What began as the blood shed to make leather garments, continued as a crimson thread throughout the pages of God's Word. Isaac was on the altar, but a ram was in the thicket ready to take the knife. The blood was on the doorposts of the Hebrew homes in Egypt as the destroyer slew every firstborn in every home—except the ones covered by the crimson stain.

The blood stream ran from the Passover lamb, to the altar of the tabernacle, to the sprinkled High Priest on the Day of Atonement. From His flogged flesh, to His thorn-pierced brow, to His nailed wrists, to His impaled side—the blood of Jesus flowed freely to cover your shame.

Jesus didn't just pay the penalty for your sin, He *became* your sin. "God made him who had no sin to be sin for us, so that in him we might become the righteousness of God" (2 Corinthians 5:21). It means that Jesus not only endured the punishment due to sinners, but He also experienced the symptoms and anguish that sin inevitably causes. Isaiah's prophecy painted the picture of the Messiah's shame 800 years before the cross: "He was despised and rejected by men.... Like one from whom men hide their faces...we esteemed him not" (Isaiah 53:3).

In the excruciating hours on the cross, Father God, in His unspeakable love for us, did two unthinkable things toward His Son. First, the Father turned His face away from His Son, as one does when disgusted. When Jesus began His ministry and was baptized, the Father spoke from heaven: "This is my Son in whom I'm well pleased." On the cross, the Father's silence communicated the opposite message: "I'm so ashamed of Him."

Second, while Jesus was on the cross, the Father lifted the cover off His only Son. He didn't even allow Jesus the clothes He had given Adam and Eve. Father God allowed Jesus Christ to hang exposed and vulnerable, not only before the watching world but also before the whole invisible realm of spiritual powers. I believe that the mocking taunts of the Roman guards or passersby held no comparison to the taunts of the invisible demons who were granted an unthinkable open season to shame the Son of God.

In the cup of suffering that Jesus drank was the poison of not only every sin ever committed, but also the shame that it evoked. In other words, on the cross, Jesus Christ was not only bearing the sin of the child molester, He also was bearing the shame of the bewildered, broken child. He was not only bearing the sin of the prostitute's adultery, He was bearing the shame of the prostitute's identity as well. He not only was bearing the sin of the alcoholic's drunkenness, but at the same time, was bearing the shame of the alcoholic's child who never invited friends home to play.

And Jesus took the shame willingly—in fact, almost eagerly—that we might be set free. *"Let us fix our eyes on Jesus, the author and perfecter of our faith, who for the joy set before him endured the cross, scorning its shame, and sat down at the right hand of the throne of God"* (Hebrews 12:2).

You don't have to keep your hornet hidden any longer.

Jesus already took the sting.

ASK   A Question to Inquire:

What hidden "hornet" is stinging me?

BELIEVE   A Principle to Ponder:

"Shame is insidious. It inflicts not only the pain of feeling really bad about ourselves, but then it begins a cycle that blocks us from taking the only steps that can help us feel better... Shame's invitation is: 'Hide from God lest you be condemned.' Jesus' invitation is: 'Seek first His kingdom and His righteousness, and all these things will be given to you as well.'"

I do not have to hide my pain from God and others in order to avoid shame. In fact, when I expose my shame to God and others, my healing can begin.

CHOOSE   A Commitment to Keep:

I choose today to quit hiding the things that I'm ashamed of. I will trust God and someone else enough to share what hurts me so that it won't keep stinging me.

pray

O God, I cannot hide from You. If I were to travel to the uttermost parts of the sea, You would be there. No more running and hiding. You are not a High Priest who is unable to sympathize with my pain. In Christ, You were despised and rejected by men and esteemed not. Thank You for the crimson flow of Your mercy that began with the skins You made to cover Adam and Eve's shame, and concluded with the blood of Jesus on the cross. I accept by faith that Jesus became sin for me that I might become the righteousness of God. Grant me new eyes that may be fixed upon Jesus, the author and perfecter of my faith who scorned the shame of the cross and reigns from on high. In Jesus' name, AMEN.

chapter *five*

shame or godly conviction?

"I don't agree with you, pastor."

Not my favorite words to hear, but I tried to listen closely.

"I think the whole premise of your *Shame Off You* series is wrong. I think we need shame. How else are we going to be deterred from continuing in our sin?"

Good question.

After half an hour of opening up, he took a deep breath and came to the core of the matter for him. "For example," he said, "I have a recurring problem with pornography. It's very difficult to curb. I think I need to feel badly about it. Being ashamed of it can help motivate me to stop. Don't I need to be ashamed of a sin like that?"

"Has it worked?" I asked. "I mean, has feeling really badly about yourself over your pornography struggle helped you?"

"Well…it has to a certain extent. It makes me more determined to stop. And sometimes, for a period of time I do stop."

"But has being ashamed ever brought you any measure of real healing?"

When he couldn't give an affirmative answer, I spoke softly, "I think shame hasn't helped you stop looking at pornography—I think shame is the reason you're tempted toward it in the first place. The pressure of feeling like you've got to do better in order to be accepted is causing the hidden anxiety in your soul. It's that anxiety that you're numbing with the fantasy of pornography. If you don't feel you measure up, that you aren't the full man that you know you are supposed to be, then you resort to two-dimensional women in a magazine or on a web page. Those nameless women always accept you. There is no risk of rejection from them. Shame isn't the cure for pornography addiction—it's the root of it."

"But shouldn't I feel badly about my sin?"

I tried to clarify. "It *is* important to despise our sin in order to repent and run to God. But that process is not shame, it's what the Bible calls conviction."[7]

encountering holiness

Twenty years ago, on an ordinary evening, I knelt to pray by the faded red couch in my small dormitory room at the University of North Carolina at Chapel Hill. I was a senior, completing two majors, English and Religion. Having discovered a love for studying Scripture and teaching others, I had mapped out in my mind a rather attractive personal plan.

It went something like this: I would pursue graduate studies in religion, and later teach Bible and theology in an academic environment. It made good sense to me. I would get to do something I loved doing. It seemed like a respectable job, and most importantly, I would still be "one of the guys."

In other words, I wouldn't be a pastor.

Had I felt the tug of a ministry call before? Perhaps. But I had tucked such promptings well beneath the surface, and had planned Life According to Alan.

Until I knelt by that faded red couch.

I don't know what urgency or depth of longing surfaced in me that day and compelled me to my knees, for it was not my usual posture of prayer. I had not knelt to seek blessing or direction or pardon. Pursuing God really wasn't in my mind at that moment.

It was more like I was being pursued.

I don't even remember the words I prayed. I just remember kneeling. And then, He was there. Like a fog that slips in on little cat feet without notice, but eventually becomes so dense that you can't move, holiness filled my dormitory room and arrested me. There were no words from the saturating Presence—just holiness. So holy, holy, holy. I felt the weight of God's glory. And as a jeweler might use a bright light and magnifier in order to detect the imperfections in a seemingly clear diamond, I knew that out of this heavy glory that had so captured me, that there was light shining on my soul.

God didn't speak.

He just opened my eyes to see what He saw.

True conviction comes not at the sound of God's displeasure in us, but at the moment He turns the light on brightly enough for us to see our imperfections. And in that moment, I did. I saw the awfulness of my sin. At least for a moment.

We could not bear to see our sin as God sees sin. The noxious odor of it, the unparalleled heartbreak of it—it's too much. For less than a blink of an eye, I saw the utter depravity of my self-consumed life with my pretty little plans for my personal comfort. At least for a moment, I felt the gigantic longings of an eternal Father, who in His greatness had (for some reason) never shown me the depth of my sin nor the futility of my plans until that instant.

It was strange. On the one hand, the revelation of my selfishness brought tears of sorrow and remorse running down my face. But at the same time, I felt that I was receiving something infinitely valuable—a gift of unspeakable proportions. Instinctively, I knew that those tears, and the broken heart behind them, were part of some, deep, cleansing stream of mercy that would wash away years of blinding self-centeredness.

So I didn't run.

Not this time. Not from the tears and not from the God who aroused them. Whatever fears I may have had about such an encounter with God simply melted away. I felt utterly safe in that cloud of holiness. Consumed with awe, I wept in His strong embrace. I grieved when I saw my selfishness in the light of His goodness and love.

Without thought, in groanings too deep for words, I crumpled at that couch-side confessional. And when I finally spoke, my tongue could only form three childlike words.

"I'm no good."

I felt compelled to recite them over and over. "I'm no good.

I'm no good. I'm no good." In those moments, God did not respond with reassurance or consolation. Nor was I looking for such a response. He knew I needed to make my confessional outpouring. So He didn't dam up my tears. Instead, God just held me and let me feel His breath as He let me say it over and over, "I'm no good. I'm no good. I'm no good."

In a strange, sweet fellowship, He and I understood His silence to be tacit agreement with my confession.

Oddly, nothing had ever felt better or more real or satisfying than those hot tears and those seemingly self-deprecating words rolling on into the mystery of God's holy presence. While I had never felt worse about my sin, I had never felt so hopeful about my future. If seeing my sin for half a second rendered me completely undone, what must it be like for an all-knowing, all-seeing God to behold my sin? And yet, He did not slay me. Instead, there I was in His embrace. He gave me the revelation of my sin that led me into uncontrollable grief and then, in the midst of that grief, He comforted me.

There, comforted by the One who had led me into my remorse, I felt more accepted than ever in my life. There I was completely naked before my Creator, completely overcome with remorse, and yet, I had absolutely no desire to hide. I knew I was utterly safe. Safer there with my tears and running nose and the embrace of the Almighty than anywhere I could be.

I have no idea how much time passed before He finally spoke. It was not audible to my ears, but it was clearly spoken from the outside of me to the inside of me. It sounded to my spirit like a gentle whisper. So sweet. So intensely personal.

"Alan, you know I'm calling you into the ministry."

The call I had so feared suddenly seemed the irresistible answer to all the longings of my life.

I just wept and nodded my head. *Oh yes*, my spirit cried. *Oh yes.*

Over the past twenty years, I have been a youth minister, attended three years of seminary, and been a lead pastor in two churches. I have had moments in which I wished I could back out or back down from this call. I have had a lot of moments in which I have made mistakes. Moments of humiliation. But I have never had one single moment in which I have doubted the whispered call next to that sofa in Stacy Dormitory. My life was changed forever. It was truly one of the greatest moments of my life. I wouldn't trade that moment weeping in God's arms for a million moments of empty laughter in the arms of the world.

I was a young man whose soul was plagued by shame. But what I experienced that day was not the curse of shame nor a bout of poor self-esteem. It was the conviction of the Holy Spirit. In that moment I could whisper with David, *"The fear of the LORD is clean, enduring forever"* (Psalm 19:9, NKJV). Since that time, I have come to cherish the conviction of the Holy Spirit every bit as much as I disdain the shame of the enemy.

Without the conviction of the Holy Spirit, we do not change and grow. It is essential that we recognize and welcome His convicting work. Surprisingly, I find that many Christians are confused about the difference between the corrosive shame that binds us and the healing conviction that frees us. It's as fundamental as recognizing the difference between the voice of Satan and the voice of God.

We need to cultivate the ability to differentiate between the voice of shame and the voice of conviction. Why? Because the one is to be rejected boldly, while the other received gladly. Thankfully, recognizing the difference is not difficult once you comprehend the unique dynamics of each.

conviction: the real thing

In Luke 15, Jesus tells the parable of the three sons.[8] The first son, the younger one, does an unthinkably disrespectful thing. In asking for his share of his inheritance, he reveals his heart's thought: *I'd be better off if my father were dead.*

After squandering his wealth in "wild living," he found himself penniless in the midst of a severe famine. Desperate simply to survive, the young Jewish man did an abominable thing when he took a job feeding ceremonially unclean pigs. As he slopped the swine, he realized he was so hungry that he was actually envious of the hogs. At least the pigs had pods to eat.

Watch the process of true conviction. First, the son recognized the poverty of his life. When he "came to his senses," he recognized that if continued, this course of life would lead to utter destruction. What he saw was his own folly. Seeing one's own folly is essential to finding the path of wisdom. "Understanding is a fountain of life to those who have it, but folly brings punishment to fools" (Proverbs 16:22). To recognize one's own folly is not shame, it's the beginning of wisdom.

In coming to his senses, it was the knowledge of his father's wealth compared to the poverty of his sin-induced predicament that began his thought process of repentance. He decided to admit he was not worthy to be called his father's son.

Why is this statement of unworthiness an expression of healthy conviction rather than toxic shame?

It's simple. *Conviction always moves us back to the Father.*

To say, "I am not worthy, so I will stay away from my Father," is shame. To say, "I am not worthy, but I will go to my Father," is conviction.

Any thought that makes you want to hide from God or from godly people is not a God thought, and is not inspired by the Holy Spirit. Shame always causes us to feel more distant from God. Conviction always makes us feel closer to God.

Throughout the course of my son Bennett's life, I have had to spank him on limited occasions. He is, simply put, a good boy. From the time he came forth from his mother's womb, I have cherished him and held him close. He trusts me profoundly. I would never harm him. I love him too intensely for words on a page. When he has willfully disobeyed and I have spanked him, he has never resisted. He has not even covered his backside with his hand. Instead, his face has fallen upon my shoulder ready for the embrace that he knows will follow.

Bennett does not get spanked unless he knows he has truly erred. He does not get sent to his room to sit in shame. Instead, he has known the error of his ways and he has cried in my arms. When you hear a voice pointing out what is wrong in you, ask yourself, *Am I being drawn to the love behind that voice or do I feel like running away?* That will begin your discernment.

As he had planned, the wandering son fell upon his father's mercy and cried: "Father, I have sinned against heaven and against you. I am no longer worthy to be called your son." In the same breath, he acknowledged his unworthiness for sonship—even as he *proved* his sonship by calling the man Father. The conviction of the Holy Spirit may cause us such remorse for our sin that, like Isaiah in the year King Uzziah died, or I in my senior year of college, we feel utterly undone. I might cry out "I'm no good, I'm no good, I'm no good," for weeks.

But in the midst of being undone, like the younger son, a strange hope prevails. A mysterious awareness arises that affirms, *Though I have made atrocious mistakes, I am not doomed. My life itself is not a mistake, but is part of God's eternal purposes.* At the same moment he acknowledged his unworthiness, marvelously, mysteriously, the younger son experienced his father's love more profoundly than ever. When real conviction comes, we do not resist acknowledging that God abhors our sin because we are filled with a greater awareness of how much He loves us. Shame emphasizes a person's total existence—"you are a mistake." Conviction focuses upon behavior that can be changed—"you have made mistakes."

When the astonishing grace of the prodigal father is lavished upon the son by means of robe, ring, sandals, and calf, something even more astonishing occurs. The unworthy son accepts the grace. "So they began to celebrate" (Luke 15:24).

Did you catch that? *They* began to celebrate. The younger son *and* the father—and anyone who would enter the party. Shame-based families seldom celebrate. The straight A report card might be met with a momentary pat on the head; but if there is one B, it is questioned.

The very nature of the kingdom of God is celebration. The

kingdom is compared to a wedding party—the greatest of Middle Eastern celebrations. The conviction of the Holy Spirit is God's way of bringing us into the kingdom in the first place. Conviction will bring a true process of remorse, but the weeping will not tarry forever, and joy will come in the morning. Shame never invites, nor allows, us into the celebration—we are too busy brooding over our inadequacy to join the party.

The older brother in the story provides a dramatic foil to the younger. The master storyteller describes the stark contrast of brothers as we see the eldest dutifully performing on the estate. This son is the kind of hard driving performer that society applauds. He works hard. He pleases others. He is conscientious. And he is full of shame.

Can you hear it? "You never gave me even a young goat...." It was a statement of low esteem disguised as criticism of his brother and his father. Instead of the radical honesty of the younger brother, who admitted his brokenness to his father, the older brother hid his feelings of unworthiness by putting others down. If someone can't enjoy your success, it most certainly means that he doesn't feel successful himself. If someone is putting you down, you can be sure it is an impoverished soul trying to prop itself up.

While the riotously sinful first son had divulged his deepest thoughts in his father's welcoming embrace, the hard-working second son was unable to even speak directly to his father. "So he called one of the servants and asked him what was going on" (v. 26). The fear of rejection keeps shame-based people from ever sharing their true longings with those who can help them the most. The younger was in a distant land but came into his father's embrace. The older was literally close by, but always figuratively distant "in the field," and emotionally unavailable to his father.

The younger son returned with the hope of being a servant, but was confirmed a son. The older, whose sonship was never in question, nonetheless perceived his life-history as one of bondage. "All these years I've been slaving for you" (v. 29). The shame-filled older son tried to manipulate his father by essentially saying, "Aren't you ashamed of yourself, Dad?" The older brother's desperate longing for attention, love, and acceptance is exposed not by a forthright, childlike admission of need, but by a manipulative technique. "You're a bad, unskilled father," is the eldest son's attempt to say, "Give me the love I need."

Tragically, the shame-filled soul doesn't comprehend the availability of the father's love, because it presumes that love is earned. *How can my younger brother be receiving so much love when he's done nothing to earn it?*

"'My son,' the father said, 'you are always with me, and everything I have is yours.'" (v. 31) *My love, my life, my heart, my affection, my material goods—all of it is always available to you.* God's love is not a reward for the righteous, it is a gift to the repentant. God's love is not acquired by living right and serving well. God's love is received only through the sweet surrender of a thirsty soul.

It is the abandonment of one's dignity and self-protection that allows lovers to experience ecstatic intimacy. It is in the abandonment of one's self-sufficiency that allows the bride of Christ to experience the sweetness of His infilling. The older brother, full of shame (but striving so hard to look worthy), is trapped and can't enjoy the party under his own nose.

	SHAME	CONVICTION
Emphasis	Person over behavior	Behavior over person
Message	"You are a bad person."	"You did a bad thing."
Self-Image	"I'm not worth even a young goat."	"I have sinned."
Emphasis	Manipulation, not mercy	Mercy, not manipulation
Message	"You'd better do something to make up for your failure."	"You can't undo it; you need to humbly ask for mercy."
Self-Image	"I have been slaving."	"I am not worthy."
Emphasis	Distance, not intimacy	Intimacy, not distance
Message	"To be all right, you'd better keep some distance in our relationship."	"You'll never really be fulfilled without intimacy; please come close."
Self-Image	I'll stay "in the field."	"I will set out and go back to my father."
Emphasis	Silent about inward hunger	Expressive about longings
Message	"If you ask for what you need most, you'll be rejected and feel even more ashamed."	"When you're in need, the best way to get help is by asking me."
Self-Image	"asked a servant"	"Father ..."
Emphasis	Busier, but no life change	Transformation, not busyness
Message	"You can't be changed, so try harder and faster."	"You don't need more activity. You need deep inner change."
Self-Image	"became angry"	"was lost and is found"
Emphasis	Avoids the celebration	Welcomes the celebration
Message	"I don't deserve a celebration, so I won't go to the party— I wish they'd quit partying and start working like me."	"I don't deserve a celebration, so it makes me all the more thankful to be invited to the party. I wish more would come."
Self-Image	"refused to go in"	"They began to celebrate."

IN THE SCHOOL OF CONVICTION

Dudley Hall summarizes the distinction between shame and conviction by telling us to imagine stepping into a dark room.[9] You step into the darkness, stumble forward, and bam! You bump your shin into a piece of furniture. Imagine a voice in the darkness: "Don't bump into the furniture, you fool." But the room stays dark. You can't see where you're going. You risk another step. Crack! You bruise your other shin and the voice returns to the darkness, "There you go again. I thought I told you to quit bumping into the furniture. Now stop it, you idiot!" But the room stays dark. Eventually, you'll either rage at the darkness or collapse in the corner helpless to move.

Now, imagine that you step into a dark room, bump into a piece of furniture and, while you're saying, "ouch," a voice says, "No need to keep on bumping into furniture—it hurts doesn't it?" Then, imagine, as the voice speaks, the light turns on. You still have a nice bruise on your shin, but you have light to see where you are going. You have the regret of foolishly bumping into the furniture, but you are relieved to have the help of the light.

The reason people reject and run from the conviction of the Holy Spirit is that their experience of the shame of the world (or in the church) has led them to believe that they'll just feel worse about themselves without improving. But what if there was more to opening yourself to the conviction of the Holy Spirit than just feeling bad? What if you found it to be the secret to discovering an abundant life?

I have come to realize that conviction is really a free education from the greatest Teacher in the world. The Holy Spirit is, first, a teacher. A good teacher has a way of showing students what they are doing wrong and then instructing them in the right way. The point of showing the students what is wrong is not for the students to feel ashamed of their mistakes, but to show them ways to improve. If the teacher is not shaming, but loving, why wouldn't I want to learn how to be more effective?

I'm a golfer. Golf, for the average hacker, is an amazingly difficult game. Every now and then, though, we hit a good shot. It's the thing that keeps us going back to the practice range with hopes of learning how to hit a good shot more often. Golfers will spend amazing amounts of time and money trying new equipment or testing out a tip from the latest golf magazine. Why do they do this? Because they hope to improve. It's not just looking at the scenery, getting the exercise, or spending time with friends that's fun. What's fun about golf is the thought of hitting the ball farther and straighter.

I read somewhere how much it costs to get a pro golfer, like Greg Norman, to spend a day at a corporate golf outing. The pro will give a few demonstrations and put on a clinic in return for a handsome fee. I was stunned to find out that some of the pros charge over $200,000 for one such day. Interestingly, the article said, Tiger Woods doesn't even do such outings. You can't get him for a day at any price.

But stretch your imagination for a moment and imagine that I, Alan Wright, because of secret reasons, have been able to obtain the personal services of Tiger Woods for a day. Tiger has agreed to be my personal coach for a full day for the sum of one half million dollars (and let's imagine I have the money to pay him).

We go to the practice tee and Tiger says, "All right Alan, let's see you hit a few." I hit a few balls and Tiger interrupts, saying, "Let's stop right here for a second. I see something in your grip that isn't right. Let me show you how to hold the club better."

Can you conceive of me (or anyone in his right mind) becoming incensed? "Hold on. Wait a minute," I say, offended. "What are you saying Tiger? You don't like the way I'm holding the club, huh? Well, who asked you? I don't need your instruction!" It's unthinkable that I would reject the teaching of the greatest golfer in the world, especially after such a high price was paid to secure him.

It must be inconceivable to God that person after person rejects the conviction of the Holy Spirit after such a high price was paid to deposit Him in our hearts. Formerly, in my shame, I saw the Holy Spirit's convicting role as something to be dreaded or avoided while I welcomed His gifts and His fruits eagerly. Now, I see conviction as the greatest, most expensive Life Coach in the cosmos, by my side, showing me what and how to change. I find myself asking much more often, "Convict me, Lord. Show me how I can grow. I don't want to bump into the same furniture tomorrow that I bumped into today. I don't want to have the same character flaws, make the same mistakes, and go down the same wrong paths. Show me Your ways, O Lord."

the third son

I spoke earlier about the parable of three sons.

The first son was a riotous sinner, broken by conviction,

fallen into his father's mercy, who discovered unparalleled celebration. The second son was a dutiful performer, bound by shame, reliant upon himself, isolated from his father's affection, who never joined the party.

The third son?

He is the Son who tells the story.

He is the Son who performed His first miracle at a party. The Son who was obedient, not for shame, but for the joy set before Him (Hebrews 12:2). He was the Son who was rejected by those He came to save, but never left His Father's embrace. He was the Son who lived in unquenchable intimacy with His Father. Even the day that He sweat blood, clawed the ground, and pleaded for relief, He did not leave His Father's embrace.

Then, in a moment, one, awful moment, the third Son hung on a cross, and there He cried: "Why have You forsaken Me?" Though the air was silent, the answer would one day be known. "I forsake You," the Father said, "so that I will not have to forsake all the others."

So the third Son hung and bore our shame. In those moments on the cross, He was both the grotesquely sinful younger brother and the dutiful, slaving older. But unlike the younger, there were no father's arms to fall into. And unlike the older, there was no assurance "you are always with me, and everything I have is yours." Instead, the third Son hung there like an unforgiven younger brother and an uninvited older brother until He breathed His last and said, "It is finished." Guilt is finished, so you can be forgiven.

To say "shame off you" isn't to say your sin is no big deal. It is, instead, to say don't confuse the voice of the enemy with that of the Advocate. God will never overlook your sin. He hates sin. But He loves you, He is for you, He is calling and waiting for you—and He will never turn you away.

Come on home. It's time to join the party.

ASK   A Question to Inquire:

When have I confused the voices of shame and conviction?

BELIEVE   A Principle to Ponder:

"Oddly, nothing had ever felt better or more real or more satisfying than those hot tears and those seemingly self-deprecating words rolling on into the mystery of God's holy presence. While I had never felt worse about my sin, I had never felt so hopeful about my future."

It's good to see my sin. Only then can I walk a better path. It is possible to be full of remorse for my mistakes while being infinitely hopeful for my future.

CHOOSE   A Commitment to Keep:

I choose today to risk going to my Father, telling Him that I have sinned, that I long for His forgiveness and I will expect Him to forgive me, hold me, and teach me.

pray

*Father, I am not worthy to be called Your son/daughter,
but I want to draw near to You today. I trust that
You will never condemn me nor turn me away.
With that confidence, I invite You to be my Teacher and
to convict me of all that is wrong in my life, so that I
can be set free and live a more abundant life. Give me
discernment to receive Your voice and to reject the voices
of shame. I want to be everything that You have made
me to be. There is no place I'd rather be than in
Your arms of love. In Jesus' name, AMEN.*

CHAPTER SIX

FOR WANT OF A MOM AND DAD

With broken hearts for forgotten children, Ernie and Ginnie Ruckert began visiting orphanages years ago. Looking for ways to help the children open up their often walled-up hearts, the Ruckerts started offering the orphans an opportunity to write poetry. What those kids have written over the years would stir you, bless you, tickle you—and sometimes, haunt you.

I've always been haunted by a particular poem of a young orphan named Juan. Juan entitled his poem "The Want of a Mom and Dad":

> Moms and dads are wonderful
> for those people
> that has a mom and a dad
> Parents that guide and teach you the right way
> Not the wrong way
> As for me

I never knew my mom
My dad drunk all the time
I don't know what it is like
to have a mom and dad
A dad to wrestle and play with
A mom to tell me everything is okay
when something is wrong
Parents that really care for me
Ones that will help me
not abuse me
I wish I had a mom and dad
Why can't I have a mom and dad
Like all the other kids?

Like all the other kids. That's Shame's motto. There is something not right about me. There is something that I don't have that I should have, and it seems that everyone else has.

I must put this plainly to you: If you grew up without a mother or father, you are automatically a target for shame. If you grew up with a mother or father who was there physically, but not there emotionally, you are automatically a target for shame. There is no source of shame more fundamental in the world than the broken family. To have anything less than a healthy mom and dad is to miss out on God's essential plan.

That's why I'm mostly haunted by the line, "A dad to wrestle with and play with / A mom to tell me everything is okay." Juan's words describe the essence of human need. They also describe the main division of labor in my own household— I wrestle and play with the kids and Anne tells them they're okay. A mom, softer than a man, lets her children feel her comfort. A dad, stronger than the woman, lets his children encounter his strength, the solidity of his manhood.

God's design is simple: We learn to trust at our mother's breast (Psalm 22:9), but we are challenged to arise to our destinies by the exhortation of a father (1 Thessalonians 2:11–12).

If we arrived on planet earth self-sufficient, we would be robbed of the most important developmental process of life—learning to trust that someone else is there for us. I gave my mother nothing when I was a baby. I spat on her shoulder, messed my diapers, and called upon her when she most wanted to sleep. But amazingly, she loved me. She cared for me and held me. Why? Unconsciously, I eventually could come to only one conclusion. She loved me because I was hers. I belonged.

The first and most important thing you could ever know about a relationship with God is that He set His affection upon you before you ever contributed anything to Him. That's what grace is. A gift. The gospel is this simple.

God says "I love you because you are Mine."

You say, "But I have nothing but spit and dirty diapers to offer You."

God says, "I love you so much that I would die for you. Even if you spit upon My shoulder, soil upon My creation, and call upon Me in the middle of the night, I will love you. Even if I have to change a thousand dirty diapers, I love you more than enough to give you everything I have."

You say, "Is there anything I must do?"

God says, "One thing only. Trust Me."

And as you place the weight of your life into the gracious

arms of God, you acknowledge that you can't feed yourself, clean yourself, and certainly can't rescue yourself. All you can do is trust. That's not only the beginning of eternal life, it's the beginning of abundant life. Shame disappears and real living begins with the grace of knowing your security in God's firm embrace.

But we're more than nursing infants, aren't we? We are called forth into our destinies by something more than the constancy of milk. The father's voice calls the child away from the warmth of the womb and into the adventure of a daring life. "Let's wrestle. Let's engage in a battle." Fathers plant dreams in children and prophetically bless the children into the realization of those dreams. They play with the child because, in the playing, the child learns that adventure, though daring, is fun.

Writing to the Christians in Thessalonica, Paul compares his ministry to both motherhood and fatherhood within just a few verses: "We were gentle among you, like a mother caring for her little children....We dealt with each of you as a father deals with his own children, encouraging, comforting and urging you to live lives worthy of God" (1 Thessalonians 2:7, 11–12).

I live for the want of a mom and dad. A mom to be gentle with me and reassure me. A dad to show me strength and give me courage to live out a great destiny.

Without a mom, I can't trust. Without a dad, I can't dream.

Without a mom, I'll build walls around my heart. Without a dad, I'll never sign up for a battle.

I need a full realization of Grace which tells me I'm accepted, no matter what. I need to be full of Truth which tells me that there is more for me to accomplish in the world.

I need enough Grace to know that I'm accepted even when I fail. I need enough Truth to know that I was made for more than milk.

the day everything changed

When I was nine years old, I presumed my life to be normal. I figured I had what other kids had, and maybe more. I had a mom and a dad. My mom allowed us to eat candy a little more often than other moms and my dad coached my pee wee football team. I had two older brothers who were pretty okay. Our family went to Myrtle Beach every year for two weeks where we would stay at the Driftwood motel, play on the beach, win stuffed animals at Skeeball, and eat in the Driftwood restaurant where Jake would wait us on us for two weeks and would make me chocolate milk (although I wished he would put more chocolate in).

Every Sunday night we would go to my grandmother and granddaddy's house, where we would watch Granddaddy watch the last hole of the golf tournament, eat a feast from Grandmother's kitchen, and watch the Wonderful World of Disney. On the way home each Sunday night, we would count cars, which we called alligators, and have a contest to see who could guess how many "alligators" we would see on the way home.

I had a mom and a dad.

My perfect world ended when I was nine because we had a "family meeting." We'd never had a "family meeting" before.

At least not like this one. Today, it is almost unbearable for me to think of the millions of children who have had to sit through their own versions of such family meetings.

I had never seen my dad cry until that night. He cried. He said he loved us kids. He said that he and Mom weren't going to be living together anymore. He would move out. He would still be able to coach my football team, but he wouldn't be there to give me "the drying machine" after my bath. He would still meet us for lunch on Saturdays, but he wouldn't be there every night at dinner to amaze us with how much he'd learned about the world during his day as a TV newsman. I could still go to Grandmother's house, but we'd never count alligators on the way home. We'd still go to the beach, but it wouldn't be my family at the Driftwood, it would be my mom, my aunt, and my cousins in a cottage.

I had a dad. Then, one day, he was gone.

My world changed forever. Shame took up residence under our roof. Oh, for the want of a mom and dad. I never remember asking myself, *What did I do wrong to lose my dad?* But I know I asked it. I never remember wondering, *What's so wrong with me that Dad doesn't want to be with me?* But I know I thought it. I never remember planning, *What must I do to win him back?* But I know I built my whole life on that goal.

He came back home a few years after that. But it was never the same. I knew something was still wrong. A few years later, when I entered high school, he left again. My brothers went to college, leaving just Mom and me. A broken, beautiful mom with a distant child who had a distant dad. O for the want of a mom and dad.

In the majority of broken homes, it is the father who is absent. No wonder that the vast majority of inmates in our prison system report an absence of a meaningful father relationship. With no father to wrestle, we will not learn to wrestle against the adversities of life, but will seek to avoid them by way of finding comfort. Too big and too embarrassed to ask for Mother's milk anymore, when pressures come, we will look for other substances to soothe us. Or we will simply withdraw from life.

For some fatherless children, like me, the prison is not a barred, cinder block room, but is a cell of shame, blockading us from the fullness of life. Where there is no father, there is no deep dream in the child. Without deep dreams, we wither into aimless orphans who either pity ourselves into ineffectiveness or who rage meaninglessly against the void of the night. O for the want of a mom and dad.

DOWN WITH THE FAVORED SON!

Rachel and Jacob's plot to steal older brother Esau's blessing by tricking Isaac into laying his aged hands upon Jacob may have demonstrated that this younger brother had always felt "unblessed" by his father. He knew the eldest son would get the blessing. How could he get his share unless he took it by deception? It must have stung Jacob's soul to realize his father's blessing was a limited commodity reserved for a favored child. And though Jacob was still limping from his wrestling match with God, and though Jacob had discovered a sense of destiny in God, the patriarch had enough shame left in his soul to make him a dysfunctional dad.

Returning to the pattern of parental favoritism of his own childhood, Jacob (or, his new name, Israel) "loved Joseph more than any of his sons..." (Genesis 37:3). With no attempt to hide his favoritism, Israel made a richly ornamented robe for Joseph to parade in front of his rejected older brothers. Having always feared missing the favor of his own father, Israel enacted the generational curse by reserving his love for only his youngest son. This exaltation of Joseph left the older brothers with orphaned hearts. While the older brothers slaved in the distant fields, only Joseph was at home in his father's intimacy.

The contrast between the son of a father's favor and the sons without a father's affection is stark.

What follows is a primer on shaming behavior. "They hated him and could not speak a kind word to him" (Genesis 37:4). Shamed people have difficulty celebrating someone else's success. Someone else's exaltation prompts feelings of rejection in the shamed person's heart. If you can't enjoy seeing someone else blessed, it probably means that you don't feel blessed yourself.

Often, we do what Joseph's brothers did next. We congregate with like-minded, shamed-based people, who will speak against the exalted or blessed one. We join judgmental fellowships that point a united finger against a common enemy. The Pharisees did not stumble over theology as much as their own hearts. Jesus' exaltation was a threat to their orphaned spirits, so, collectively, they pointed their finger at the Nazarene.

When Joseph had a great dream, "they hated him all the

more" (Genesis 37:5). Though the dream was not ultimately about his siblings' humiliation but about their salvation, the brothers couldn't stand it. Instead of having their own dreams, they could envision the torment ending only by ending the focal point of their torment. Instead of courageously going to their father and beseeching the intimacy their souls really craved, the older brothers allowed their shame to intensify...until it boiled over.

Unfathered, we do not move proactively into the world to make our own positive impact. Instead, the orphaned heart is forever responding to someone else's dream—either to defeat it or to co-opt it for personal gain. Unconvinced of their own places in God's eternal plan, the rejected older siblings could think of nothing but eliminating Joseph.

When we have enough deep-seated shame, we will always devise a plot to destroy the favored one. The alcoholic husband, instead of courageously facing his inward inadequacy, blames the woman and, through abuse or divorce, destroys her. But removing the favored one never heals our inward shame. It only creates more of the same.

Notice the steps of these brothers' shame-filled scheme. "They stripped him of his robe—the richly ornamented robe he was wearing..." (Genesis 37:23). If I feel naked and exposed, I will eventually try to strip someone else of his covering. Assuming the beautiful robe to be some sort of magical empowerment to Joseph, they removed it first, as if to say, "Let's see if superman can fly without his cape."

Next, "they took him" (v. 24). They made him their hostage.

If we are in a prison of shame, so shall you be. If we can't be free, then we will put you into bondage as well.

"And threw him into the cistern" (v. 24). If I can't feel higher about myself, I must make you lower. When others put you down, they prove that they, themselves, do not feel high. *Our lives are in the pits, Joseph. See what it feels like in the pit.*

When a caravan came by, they found an answer better than murder. "Come, let's sell him to the Ishmaelites.... So when the Midianite merchants came by, his brothers pulled Joseph up out of the cistern and sold him for twenty shekels of silver to the Ishmaelites" (vv. 27–28).

Shame ultimately objectifies a person. You are not valued for your personhood. You are not valued for relationship. You are worth only what you can do for me. Slaves are owned and valued for their productivity. But sons and daughters are adopted and valued for the love to be shared. Slavelike, the older brothers had no relationship with their father. So they sold the only true son as a slave.

Prostitution is a symbol of ultimate shame, *I am only worth what someone will pay for me, so I might as well sell myself.* Fatherless children are tempted to prostitute themselves in a thousand different ways. Every concession of integrity in order to gain the "payment" of acceptance from others is an unseen prostitution of our souls. You and I are not commodities for sale to the highest bidder! We are not objects that can be auctioned off on the slave block of society to a world that wants us for our performance but not our hearts. Shame off you when the world strips you of what is precious to you, rejects you, puts you down, and sells you to the passersby!

Remember whose you are, favored child of Father God.

The Christian's life is a Joseph life. In Christ, you are favored with your own robe of anointing, laden with your own unique gifts, and shaped into your own unique design. Destined to realize world-changing dreams, those healed of shame live in stark contrast to Joseph's older brothers.

Though stripped of his coat, Joseph is never stripped of his dreams. Though thrown into a pit, Joseph is never in the pits. Though sold as a slave, Joseph never thinks nor acts like a slave. The intimacy of his father's affection had worked a security into Joseph's soul so deep that he remained undaunted by the desperate actions of his brothers.

I marvel at three remarkable moments in the story of Joseph. They mark the beauty of a shame-free life.

1. I marvel at the moment Joseph resisted temptation.

Having been sold into slavery, Joseph rises to a place of prominence under his master, Potiphar. Potiphar's wife lusted for the young, well-built, Hebrew and attempted, day after day, to lure Joseph to her bed. Resisting even her seductive grasp, Joseph "left his cloak in her hand and ran out of the house" (Genesis 39:12). For any man to resist the seduction of a woman is a testimony to deep, inward security. But for Joseph—a slave, a man with so little to lose, with so many disappointments and pressures—it was a huge milestone in his life.

Sometimes we try to deceive ourselves with reasoning something like this: "I will resist temptation because I already feel bad enough about myself, and I don't want to feel worse."

It just doesn't work.

We simply cannot harness our shame in order to defeat temptations born of shame. As I learned from a friend struggling with pornography, the feelings of self-worthlessness only serve to promote the temptation.

I asked my friend how his poor self-image impacted his ability to face temptation. His response was beautifully candid, "When I'm feeling really bad about myself and I turn to pornography, it's not that I'm unaware that it's wrong or unaware that it won't really help me. It's just that, when I feel that worthless already, I figure I might as well sin."

In other words, "If I'm already at a low place, I might as well just do base things, because that's who I am."

The way that we resist temptation is neither through harnessing shame nor through pumping up self-will. The way to avoid sin is to become so secure that we will not need the sin and, for that reason, the thought of the sin becomes utterly inconsistent with our self-image.

"With me in charge," [Joseph] told her, "my master does not concern himself with anything in the house; everything he owns he has entrusted to my care. No one is greater in this house than I am.... How then could I do such a wicked thing and sin against God?" (Genesis 39:8–9).

Please hear me on this: *Joseph's resistance to temptation was not rooted in extraordinary will power, but in extraordinary self-worth.* "No one is greater in this house than I...." The favor of the father, the dream in his heart, and the security of belonging to God made it unthinkable to mix his blessed status with the sin of adultery which, in Joseph's mind, would be fitting only to someone of lesser estate.

The temptress says, *You're a slave. Your life is going nowhere fast. Your only chance at happiness or advancement is through the pleasures of sin and the deception of others. Enjoy the moment of pleasure; it will temporarily make you forget that you are a slave whose life is slipping away. Come to bed with me and you will feel alive again.*

The only way that we can avoid the temptation to settle for a perversion of real love is to have real love. Once, when Abigail was about three, I was kissing her cute little face when I paused to ask my wife, "Do you think I can kiss Abby too much?"

My wise wife smiled and responded, "I think every kiss she gets from you now is one less kiss she'll look for from a teenage boy one day."

You should have seen me kiss her then! I became a human kissing machine!

Joseph's ability to decline the invitation of lust was rooted in the deep well of love he had known from his infancy. The beloved son, therefore, says no to the temptress because the outward purity of his life mirrors the purity of the gold in his own soul.

2. I marvel at Joseph's immediate acceptance of Pharaoh's offer.

After he had been unjustly imprisoned for over two years, Joseph was presented with an astounding offer. The great king over the mighty Egyptian empire told him, "I hereby put you in charge of the whole land of Egypt" (Genesis 41:41).

Can you imagine? Here was a young man who had been

utterly rejected. Stripped of his dignity. Thrown in a cistern. Sold to passersby. Unjustly accused. Forgotten in prison. Forsaken by family. Without any earthly reason to hope.

Wouldn't most people give up?

How many people can go from pit to pinnacle in the blink of an eye and thrive? How many people can move from the castle's dungeon to its throne in the same day and sit on the throne as if they had always been there?

I marvel that Joseph could accept such a lofty position without trembling. I marvel that he didn't fear the responsibility. I marvel at how readily he received the ring and robe and chain. It amazes me that while on that throne, Joseph didn't abuse his power by abusing others, but exercised his office with dignity and maturity.

Perhaps the worst calamity of shame upon our souls is not that it puts most of us in the gutters or the rehab centers, but that it keeps us from fulfilling the destiny we have been given by God. We cannot fulfill the assignment of our lives to be a blessing to others if we cannot allow ourselves to be blessed. Until we are rid of shame-based thinking that tells us that someone else could do the job better, that someone else's idea should be used, or that someone else is better qualified, then we are not fully available to God.

True submission requires us trusting God in pits and on pinnacles. Most shame-based people can accommodate a prison, but can you take a throne? It is not humility to say, "Aw, shucks, I think someone else should be on that throne," it is shame. It is not pride to say, "Yes, I will wear the robe and the ring," it is wholeness.

3. I marvel that Joseph could so readily forgive.

This incident in Joseph's biography transcends them all. When his brothers were finally reunited to Joseph after all those years thinking him dead, they, though unaware of Joseph's identity, were utterly at his mercy. Joseph's childhood dream literally came to pass as the brothers knelt before him.

In Joseph's tongue was life and death. One word, one gesture, and the starving Hebrew brothers would be destroyed by a host of armed guards. But Joseph forgave them, blessed them, and made them belong. "So then, don't be afraid. I will provide for you and your children" (Genesis 50:21).

We can provide for someone else to the extent that we know our own wealth. Perhaps the greatest reason that God wants to heal your shame is that He has a place of influence for you in the cause of heaven.

He has a throne with your name on it.

No, it may not be a publicly acknowledged position. It may not be with outward adornment. But the God of the universe has an important post in His service that He wants you to fill. As with Joseph, He has a place of influence for you. And in that secure, prominent place, He wants you to forgive, bless, and redeem those in a famine land. No current pit can prevent God from destining you for a future pinnacle. No past failure or imprisonment should ever prevent you from saying yes to the throne that God grants you.

The gospel of Jesus Christ has extraordinary parallels with Joseph's story. It is the account of a favored Son, the One upon whom the dove descends and the Father declares, "This is my Son, upon whom My favor rests." The favored Son knows nothing but the intimacy of the Father and the fullness of the Father's love.

The Father demonstrates His favor upon Jesus to all the world by the richness of the anointing placed upon the Son's shoulders. The Son unashamedly declares the Father's favor upon His life, "As the Father has loved me, so have I loved you" (John 15:9). The Son unashamedly confesses His intimacy with the Father, "I am in the Father and the Father is in me" (John 14:11), and boldly shares His dream, "He has anointed me to...preach deliverance to the captives" (Luke 4:18). And like His Old Testament forerunner, Jesus' dream is mocked, and a conspiracy arises to destroy the Dreamer.

Falsely accused, wrongly punished, and with more than enough power to destroy those who have persecuted Him, Jesus, like Joseph, does not wield His authority to punish, but to forgive. The dream that so threatened His persecutors became, in reality, the only way out of famine and certain death. "Father, forgive them" (Luke 23:34).

God offers you food in your famine, even though you have rejected Him. "Come to Me, all you who labor and are heavy laden, and I will give you rest" (Matthew 11:28). You need not strive any longer, He tells us. Here, rest in My arms.

And there, in those arms, El Shaddai feeds you, holds you, comforts you, and finally, you learn to trust. God not only comforts you as with a mother's love, He adopts you into His very family circle.

"I will not leave you as orphans."

John 14:18

"How great is the love the Father has lavished on us, that
we should be called children of God!"

1 JOHN 3:1

Jesus Christ, full of grace and truth, becomes your Brother,
and you become a "coheir" with Christ, never to be orphaned
again.

WOOING the ORPHAN HEART

Only as I begin to comprehend the vastness of the love Father
God poured upon me by adopting me as His child, only then can
I dream great dreams, resist temptations, accept lofty assignments,
forgive those who hurt me, and bless the starving world.

In ancient Rome, the process of adoption allowed a free
man to secure the child of slaves and forgive all debts to the
child and the family. Once the debt had been forgiven, the
Roman magistrate would declare the child to be a member of
the new family. Once adopted, the child could never again be
sold as a slave.

Culminating many months of preparations, pleadings,
and paperwork, my cousin Jan was on a plane over the
Atlantic Ocean on America's day of tragedy, September 11,
2001. Her traveling companion was Sasha, her new, four-
year-old daughter. Adopted from a Russian orphanage, Sasha
spoke no English, scarcely knew her new mom, and had no
idea what sort of life was in store for her. Though Jan and
Sasha had to be rerouted to Ireland for an overnight stay, they
were soon allowed back to the United States.

The Monday after Sasha arrived, Jan brought her to our house to play with our then three-year-old, Abigail. We greeted Sasha with presents and smiles. It was exciting and heartbreaking to see her open the packages because Sasha wasn't able to comprehend that the dolls and toys were *her* things. No child "owned" anything in her communal orphanage. If there was any kind of toy at her orphanage, it was shared property. Not knowing how to explain to her the nature of a love gift, we just kept gesturing for her to play with her new stuff. But if you touched "her" toy, she'd push your hand away. She figured if you touched it, you might take it; and if you took it, she might never see it again.

Soon she and Abby ventured into the backyard to play. Can you imagine watching a newly adopted orphan pump her legs on a swing set for the first time? Can you envision a four-year-old dipping her toes into a sandbox for the first time? Can you imagine a resident of a bleak orphanage suddenly finding the free reign of a green, grassy backyard?

When it came time to leave, Sasha wouldn't. No amount of motioning, luring, or pleading would get Sasha to leave our back yard. Finally, I asked Jan, "How will we ever get her into your car?"

"I don't know," Jan said. "You see, this is the most fun she's had in her whole life. I don't have any way to explain to her that this is the way it's going to be from now on. As far as Sasha knows, once she leaves, she'll never be able to come back."

Sasha had no ears to hear the truth that would set her free, *You're adopted now. You will see greater things than this. You won't be abandoned ever again.* We had no language with which to assure her of her new status. Sasha was a daughter, but her mentality was still that of an orphan. Her position had changed, but her mind was still confined.

There we are, with Sasha, paralyzed to follow the Father who wants to move us deeper into our destinies. God found us in our remote and bleak orphanages and brought us into a land flowing with milk and honey. But fearful of losing what we have, we refuse to follow Him fully.

In this increasingly fatherless nation, our orphan hearts will be healed of their shame only as we grow into the assurance of our adoption as children of Father God. Your home may have been broken. You may have cried with Juan, Oh, for the want of a mom and dad. You might have missed a dad to wrestle with you or a mom to tell you everything is okay. But there is One who sought you out in your remote orphanage. He selected you. He laid the plans, fought through the opposition, paid the price, and came to make you His. All debts were forgiven you. And Jesus Christ, the Magistrate, declared you to be a child of God. No longer a slave, you can never be auctioned off again.

Once you are adopted, nothing can snatch you from your Father or your family. You belong—forever. So enjoy your gifts, no need to fear losing them. Romp in the yard. Wriggle your toes in the sandbox. Swing high. Dream dreams. Resist temptations. Receive thrones. Forgive sinners. Bless the world. But do not fear, child of God, "Nothing can separate you from the love of God in Christ Jesus."

Shame off you—your family isn't broken—you're a member of the most unified family in the world. May every Juan discover the joy of being in God's family.

ASK   A Question to Inquire:

What have I missed the most—the comfort of a mom or the strength of a dad? What have I missed that needs to be filled?

BELIEVE   A Principle to Ponder:

"Only inasmuch as I comprehend the vastness of that love demonstrated in my adoption as a child of Father God can I dream great dreams, resist temptations, accept lofty assignments, forgive those who hurt me and bless the starving world."

Though I may not have had a healthy mom and a dad, I do not have to live with an orphan mentality. My adoption into God's family is more than enough to heal me and set me free.

CHOOSE   A Commitment to Keep:

I choose today to let the joy and security of my adoption by Father God replace the emptiness of my orphan past.

PRAY

O God, You are my comfort and my strength.
I am complete in You. You know how I have suffered the
desolations of an orphan. But You, O God, have adopted
me into Your very own family. Grant me a deeper

assurance of my belonging so I will never feel like an orphan. Where I have learned to mistrust, teach me about Your faithfulness. Where I have felt rejected, show me Your acceptance. Then, out of the enormity of Your love, speak a deep dream into my heart that I might be a blessing to a starving world. In Christ, AMEN.

CHAPTER SEVEN

escape for the scapegoat

O nce a year, my city offers a public service called "Large Item Pickup." For one week, city residents are allowed to place bulky items like old gas grills, lawn mowers, or furniture at the curbside for city trucks to pick up and haul off to the landfill. It's supposed to be a community service that provides a good opportunity for residents to get rid of old junk that's too big to fit into a trash can.

That's what it's supposed to be.

But what it actually has become is a hilarious junk swap week.

The first year I experienced "Large Item Pickup" I put some junk at the curb and was amazed that it was gone that same day! *Boy, the city workers are so on the ball,* I thought. *They've already picked up my bulky items!* But strangely, my next door neighbor still had some junk at his curbside. As I gazed up and down my road, I noticed it was dotted by pickup trucks along the way. What I realized, of course, was that the city workers hadn't picked up my things, somebody else had!

Last year, I had put some stuff out at the street, including an old lawn mower. I was in the front yard when one of the scavengers called out to me, "Excuse me, does this lawn mower work?" I approached her and began telling her that, indeed, the mower worked fine. It was just old and had a broken handle. She looked it over a bit longer, trying to decide whether to take it. I reiterated, "It really does work." *Wait a minute,* I chuckled to myself, *what am I doing? I'm out here trying to talk someone into taking my trash!*

I've often thought of writing an editorial for our local paper to propose eliminating "Large Item Pickup" from the sanitation department's annual budget and just calling it "Large Item Swap" week.

Anyway, picture it for purposes of analogy. I have a gas grill on my back patio. No one, except a thief, is going to come to my back patio during "Large Item Pickup" and take my gas grill. In fact, no one is even going to ring my doorbell and inquire, "Is that gas grill on your back patio available for 'Large Item Pickup?'" Even a simple child would clearly understand that, no, the grill on my back patio is not available for anyone to "pick up."

However, the moment I take a grill from the back patio and put it on the curbside, everyone knows that it's available for public consumption. It's clear to everyone. Stuff on the curbside is available. Stuff not on the curbside is not available. There's a clear boundary line.

No one has to put up a "No Trespassing" sign or an electric fence to communicate what's "in bounds" and what's not. You can see easily into my front yard. There is no concrete wall or other barrier preventing people from viewing the flower planters on my front porch stoop or my garden hose. It's all in plain view, but everyone understands that those things are mine and that they would become available to others only if I put them at the curb. If a curbside scavenger started encroaching into my front yard and helping himself to my garden hose, then I would, of course, quickly let him know that he had stepped over the line.

Our lives have to be like that.

personal boundaries

You and I need personal boundaries in our lives—boundaries that are clear to everyone. No, this doesn't mean we have to build walls around our hearts or put cold barriers between others and us. In fact, it's all right for people to see into our lives and even to view some of the treasures inside.

But they have to know what's available and what's not.

They need to know that we share our "stuff," especially our "large items," only when we choose to do so.

In healthy families, children learn about boundaries from their parents. At the simplest levels, children learn that they can have privacy. They come to understand that certain body parts are not for others to touch, that they don't have to share their toys unless they want to, that they can keep some things confidential, and that their desires are valid.

As I'm writing, my five-year-old and nine-year-old are in nearby rooms. Just a few moments ago, I heard Bennett say to his little sister, "Abby, leave me alone!"

I didn't particularly like the tone in his voice, but I didn't mind him saying it. It would be a mistake for me to rebuke Bennett for wanting some space. I'm not going to tell him that he has to allow Abby to be around him all the time.

Similarly, if my children know I'm in my office working, they'll want to poke their head in and ask me a question like, "When are you going to stop writing and come play with us?" I'm glad they feel comfortable approaching me and I'm glad they want me to play with them. But I've had to explain that, for the time being, I'm writing. I further explain that, after a while, I'll stop; and at that time, I'll be available to them. In normal day-to-day interactions like that, children learn that no person can be available to you all the time, and that we must learn to respect a person's boundaries.

In shame-based homes, healthy boundaries don't emerge naturally. Parents who don't have healthy boundaries themselves make too much of their emotional life available to the child. The emotionally distraught parent makes the child a confidante to sooth his or her loneliness. To reveal too much of my inward emotional life to my children with the hope that they will be a comfort to me is to violate the child.

Children develop boundaries only as they mature. With this in mind, the parent is responsible for setting boundaries on behalf of the children when they are young. The parent's role is to protect the child from invasive forces like scary movies or unhealthy touch.

Abuse or molestation is the most tragic boundary violation. It teaches the child, "My body is not my own; it exists to please others." As a result, the sexually molested child usually becomes promiscuous in adolescence. The promiscuous adolescent may not enjoy sex at all, in fact, may despise it. But he or she can't seem to stop because of a deep-seated "belief" that I exist to please others.

When healthy boundaries are not present, a person, in effect, puts way too much stuff on the curbside for "Large Item Pickup." Passersby assume that they can help themselves to the "stuff." The stuff we put on the curbside of our lives can be such large items as our sexuality, our time, our emotional energy, our money, and our talents.

A precious lady in my church once told me, "I feel like people are walking around with a giant plug, and when they see me, they plug in and zap all my energy."

Ever feel that way?

Do people just assume they can presume upon your time? Do others know they can *always* count on you to help them out? Do people seem to take advantage of your generosity? Do you sometimes find yourself wishing that you hadn't given your time, your energy, your resources, your body, or your secrets to someone? Do people borrow money from you and not pay it back? Do you have grown children who are still living off your generosity but not taking responsibility for their lives? Do you have a hard time saying "no"—and feel guilty if you do?

If so, its time to escape the scapegoat syndrome.

a tale of two goats

There were two goats on the mysterious Hebrew Day of Atonement.

We point to and preach about the goat that was slaughtered to pay for the sin of the people. We know that goat. Its blood is the payment for our debt—the way of salvation. Aaron took its blood behind the veil, sprinkled it on the atonement cover in the Most Holy Place and, for the moment, for a season, the sin-debt was paid.

We know about the innocent animal whose blood was shed on the Day of Atonement, because we remember the blood of the Passover lamb on the doorposts of the Hebrew huts in Egypt. We preach about the blood that was shed because it foreshadows the heart of our story—worthy is the Lamb that was slain for us.

I've always known about the goat whose blood was shed.

But I never heard a sermon about the second goat.

"From the Israelite community he is to take two male goats…. He is to take the two goats and present them before the LORD at the entrance to the Tent of Meeting. He is to cast lots for the two goats—one lot for the LORD and other for the scapegoat. Aaron shall bring the goat whose lot falls to the Lord and sacrifice it for a sin offering. But the goat chosen by lot as the scapegoat shall be presented alive before the LORD to be used for making atonement by sending it into the desert as a scapegoat….

"When Aaron has finished making atonement for the Most Holy Place, the Tent of Meeting and the altar, he shall bring forward the live goat. He is to lay both hands on the head of the live goat and confess over it all the wickedness and rebellion of the Israelites—all their sins—and put them on the goat's head. He shall send the goat away into the desert in the care of a man appointed for the task. The goat will carry on itself all their sins to a solitary place; and the man shall release it in the desert." (Leviticus 16:5, 7–10, 20–22)

The first goat was payment for the debt of sin, bearing the punishment that the people deserved. The first goat bought forgiveness. At least for one more day, one more season, God would not release His wrath against His people for their rebellion. He wouldn't destroy the sinners—the goat would be their substitute. By God's grace, the demand for justice would be temporarily fulfilled by spilling the blood of the first goat.

The first goat was a gracious provision from a gracious God.

But one goat wasn't enough.

Why? Because even though the debt was paid, the haunting memory of failure continued. The debt was gone with the first goat, but the shame lingered on.

the second most important question

If you haven't asked it, there is no more urgent question than "What must I do to be saved?"

But there was a second goat. And there is a second question. Not as urgent as the first, perhaps, but very, very important nonetheless.

"What must I do to be healed?"

It is not enough for my guilt to be gone. I must find a way to be cleansed of the haunting memory of my repeated failures.

If I were about to be evicted because I was five months behind on my mortgage payments and, at the last moment, a benefactor paid the debt for me, I would be overjoyed. But it would not be enough. I would still be haunted by the knowledge that I had allowed myself into the predicament in the first place. I might be consumed with feelings of guilt even though, legally speaking, I wasn't guilty anymore. My legal standing might have changed, but my self-perception might have not. In fact, if my debt was paid, but my thought life was unhealed, I might be so consumed with the memory of my failure that I could hardly enjoy living in the house that my benefactor had so generously rescued for me.

Paul Tournier tells of a doctor who had two sons, one of whom suffered a disability. Concerned about the disabled son's feelings of inferiority, they seldom corrected or disciplined him when he disobeyed. They figured their leniency was a demonstration of grace to build the boy's self esteem.

Sometime later, however, when they employed a psychotherapist to help the son accept his disability, the analyst reported to the father: "You have weighed down the mind of this child while thinking that you were lightening the load. When he acted foolishly he ought to have been punished in order to make recompense; in that way the account would have been settled. But because of your indulgence he has kept within himself the weight of his guilt, even though you have forgiven him."[10]

The Hebrew people, like all people, faced the same predicament. It wasn't enough to be forgiven their debt—they needed to resolve their inward feelings of guilt. They needed one goat to resolve their guilt. They needed another goat to bear their shame.

Most Christians I know have received the gift of Christ as payment for their sins, but have *not* received the gift of Christ as the bearer of their shame. This explains why so many believers, though knowing Jesus died for them, still feel guilty. It explains why Christians, who are free from the law, are still trying to earn their way into the heaven they have already been promised. It explains why a person can be a born-again, bound-for-eternal-glory child of God, and be meaner than a junkyard dog. And it explains why we put too much of our "large items" on the curbside of life.

There are scapegoats in the sandlot on the school ground. *"Hey, everyone, look at Johnny; he can't make it across the monkey bars—ha, ha, ha. Look at Johnny; he throws a ball like a girl. Ha, ha, ha. Look at Johnny; nobody ever picks him for his team. Ha, ha, ha."* Ashamed of our own inadequacies against the demands of life, we'll put our shame on Johnny. At least we're not as weak and slow as he is.

There are scapegoats in families. Sometimes it's the middle child. He is not as perfect as the firstborn. Not as cute as the baby. He seems to always get into trouble. If the family isn't happy, it must be someone's fault. *Let's blame the middle child. The problem isn't my parenting, it's my rebellious middle child. The problem's not our marriage, it's our middle child. If anything goes wrong, I'm sure he's in the middle of it. Let's praise our older child—see how smart he is? Let's pet our youngest child—see how cute she is? But let's persecute our middle child. After all, someone's got to be responsible for this mess we're in.*

There are scapegoats in marriages. Someone to shame. It's your fault. You're too fat. You're too dumb. You have too many friends. You don't have enough friends. You're gone too much. You're hovering around me too much. One spouse loses all the arguments and, over time, feels lower and lower and lower, until, finally, she will take just about anything—even a fist.

There are scapegoats in the workplace. Anxiety grows amidst the uncertainty of the times. We hear that layoffs are coming. I fear for my job. Sales have been down. And I think…it's Sue's fault. She's the weakest link. Talk behind her back. Shift the shame. Get her fired. I don't feel secure, but at least I'm not poor Sue.

If our sins are paid for by the first goat's blood, but our shame is unhealed, we will always be looking for another goat. That's why wounded people wound people. That's why ashamed people shame people. That's why we need Jesus not only to save us, but also to heal us. Isaiah foretold it. Because we needed a savior, it "was the LORD's will to crush him and cause him to suffer…" and to make "his life a guilt offering" (Isaiah 53:10). Because we needed someone to bear our shame, "he took up our infirmities and carried our sorrows" (v. 4).

why me?

Ever feel like someone else's scapegoat? Consider the sequence of events for the second goat on the Hebrew Day of Atonement. It might be painful, but look for yourself in the drama.

"He is to cast lots for the two goats—one lot for the
LORD and the other for the scapegoat." (Leviticus 16:8)

It seems so arbitrary, doesn't it? How was it decided that
you'd be a scapegoat? Doesn't make sense, does it? It's because
it isn't about you—it's about others' needs to put their shame
on you.

Perhaps the greatest, best-loved cartoon of all time is the late
Charles Schultz' "Peanuts." It is, essentially, the continuing saga
of a scapegoat. A boy with a zigzagged shirt named Charlie
Brown serves as the object of all the kids' scorn and shame.
"You're a blockhead, Charlie Brown." Charlie Brown has fully
internalized the shame and, though managing his way through
life, is essentially depressed and fully expects life to turn out sour
at every turn.

But why Charlie Brown? In actuality, he's a likeable fellow
who seems at least as bright as the rest of the characters. Even
when he gets the spindly little Christmas tree for the Christmas
play, there is something endearing about his heart for the underdog. Charlie Brown is the scapegoat not because he is dumber,
less gifted, or less likeable. He's the scapegoat for only one dis-
cernable reason: The other kids decided so. The simple fact that
the whole Peanuts gang agrees to put down, pick on, and blame
Charlie Brown *makes* him the scapegoat.

Why are you being made a scapegoat?

Because you are there.

It's nothing more than the casting of lots. Will you please
reconsider whether you are supposed to be bearing the shame of
the gang? Could it be that there really is no reason at all for you

to be bearing the brunt of someone else's shame? Isn't it possible that it's just a matter of convenience? Others feel ashamed of their deep inadequacies and there you are. You're no more deserving of the role of scapegoat than anyone else. You're just…available.

There is nothing inherent within the Hebrew scapegoat that makes it the scapegoat! It's just an ordinary goat upon whom the lot fell. Why some despised racial minority in America? Why the Jews in Hitler's Germany? No reason. Nothing inherent in them at all. Just the power of a gang to cast the lot and name a scapegoat.

> "He is to lay both hands on the head of the live goat
> and confess over it all the wickedness and rebellion of
> the Israelites…and put them on the goat's head."
> (Leviticus 16:21)

We don't lay ceremonial hands upon our scapegoats, but we have many ways to make the transfer, don't we? Name-calling— "You're a loser." Gossip—"I can't believe what she was wearing! Did you see that outfit?" Mockery—"You're a joke." Cursing— "Damn you. Go to hell."

Christians have found religious words to make the transfer of shame, "We really need to be praying for Susan, did you hear about her affair?" Translated, *I don't feel good about my own life or marriage, but at least I didn't have an affair.*

Like the ceremonial hands upon the goat's head, people will attempt to put things into *your* head. You can't stop them from speaking. You can't stop them from shaming. But you do have a choice as to what you allow in your head.

In Paul's list of the spiritual armor issued to every Christian is the helmet of salvation (Ephesians 6:17). The head is the command center of the body. How we think determines how we live. Our over-availability to others is a symptom of shame-based thinking and is rooted in a lack of assurance that our salvation, freedom, and worth have been bought completely by Jesus Christ. The helmet of salvation symbolizes the depth of assurance that Paul had—"Nothing can separate me from the love of God in Christ Jesus" (Romans 8:38–39).

a ticket to the wilderness

> "He shall send the goat away into the desert.... The goat will carry on itself all their sins to a solitary place; and the man shall release it in the desert." (Leviticus 16:21–22)

The scapegoat is relegated to an unfertile place—a desert. It must remain in a solitary place—a wilderness.

Those who lay hands on the scapegoat don't want to see the animal who bears their shame. The purpose of the Day of Atonement ceremony was to shift the shame. If the goat returns to society, it displays the people's shame before them again. It's because we can't stand the sight of our own shame that we have designated a scapegoat in the first place.

Ever notice that what you like least in someone else is what you like least about yourself? Whatever bothers you most about someone else is probably what bothers you most about yourself.

I get so frustrated when my wife is late—especially if she's holding us both up. "What a joke," my friends would tell you. "Talk about the pot calling the kettle black!" I've built a notorious reputation for lateness that has caused good friends to lie to me about the starting times of meetings to get me there on time! Whatever bothers you about someone else is probably not that person's flaws, but your own.

When the frustrated parent says to the child, "I've had it with you—go to your room and don't come out until I tell you," it's not for the child's sake, it's for the parent's. The parent doesn't want to see the reminder of his own impatience. He doesn't want to face his own inability to have intimacy with his child.

Sometimes a parent needs a little distance to simmer down, but "Go to your room" is not an effective disciplinary tool. Discipline should be an act of deep intimacy, never isolation. In isolation, the child becomes a scapegoat in a wilderness. In isolation, the child makes inward conclusions, *"I'm not wanted in my parent's presence. There's something wrong with me. I must bear my own shame."*

We instinctively know that the only viable scapegoat is an isolated one. That's why the gang doesn't invite Charlie Brown to the parties. No one sends him valentines. We need our scapegoats to bear our shame in isolation so that we can pretend that a genuine transfer has taken place. When the "problem teenager" is once again chastised, he storms out of the house. The parents act frustrated again by his leaving, but intuitively, know that he must leave in order to bear the shame in isolation.

When the husband loses his temper and yells at his wife, he walks out with the words, "I can't stand the sight of you." If

I project my ugliness onto you, then I'll tell you to "Get out of my face." If I need you to "get out of my face," I'm revealing that I can't stand looking into a mirror. If I project my shame onto you, then the sight of you will seem offensive to me.

Who constantly takes the "large items" of your soul and leaves you with nothing? Who has rejected you? Who has sent you to the desert? Who has isolated you? Could it be that his rejection of you is a rejection of himself? Could it be that her abandonment of you is not because of *your* ugliness but because of what she dislikes about *herself*?

Everything works to keep the scapegoat isolated. Families unconsciously conspire to isolate the scapegoat and form unwritten "rules" that keep the shame hidden. The battered and bruised child is told, "If any of your teachers ask about the bruises, tell them you fell." In the office, nobody takes up for the scapegoat for fear of losing his own job, so the scapegoat has no colleague. In the school house, if a "normal" kid sits with the "uncool" kid, he might gain guilt by association. Fearing being scapegoated also, the "normal" kid leaves the "uncool" kid in isolation.

The most powerful and important thing a scapegoat can do is refuse isolation. Coming into relationship can bring miraculous change.

ticket out of the wilderness

For a couple of years, my wife and I hosted a home group for young adults. A college student from another city had somehow heard about our young adult group and phoned to tell me that his sister, whom I'll call Cynthia, lived in my city and might like to come to the home group if someone would call her. Not long thereafter, I called her. We had a pleasant conversation in which I not only invited her to home group but also to church. She seemed happy to receive the invitations, and we made plans for her to meet my wife at the beginning of the service and sit with her during church. The next week, Cynthia came to the young adult group, began making friends, growing spiritually, and loving God deeply.

One Friday evening, about a year after Cynthia had been coming, we had an especially small gathering consisting of those who had grown closest over the past year. There was a wonderful spirit of trust and intimacy in the room and so I deviated from the Bible study I had planned and invited people to share their spiritual stories. Cynthia said that she'd like to share.

"I grew up in church and was a Christian, but before coming here, I was away from God. Part of my journey is that I've struggled with my sexual identity. I experimented with some female friends in college. I didn't feel 'normal' and became especially lonely right after college. I wasn't plugged into any church and became more involved in homosexual relationships.

"About a year ago, on a Sunday afternoon, I was sorting out my life and trying to decide about my identity. That afternoon, I was in the process of making the conclusion, 'Okay, I'm a lesbian,' when the phone rang. It was Alan calling to invite me to this home group. That's when I met you guys and my life began to change."

Among her friends, growing in Christ, Cynthia was no

longer isolated, and she discovered her identity in Christ, not in homosexual relationships. She's now involved in significant leadership roles in our church.

faLse aLaRms

The scapegoat is essentially a person without clear boundaries. For people with deep shame, it is very difficult to sort through an appropriate level of availability to others. It seems almost impossible to say no to anyone with a legitimate need. For years, I not only found it difficult to tell anyone that I wasn't available, but when I did summon up the courage to say no, I'd spend more energy feeling guilty about "letting the person down" than I would have spent helping them.

When the phone would ring and someone would be on the other end with a need, a silent alarm would go off inside me. A quiet panic would fill my heart because I felt that if I became aware of a need, then I would feel responsible to take care of it. What a frightening way to live! Every need from every human being became a silent alarm blaring in my soul.

We have a security system in our house now. Recently, the alarm went off in the middle of the night. My adrenalin started pumping, blood rushed to my vital organs to ready me for a fight (or a fast flight), and stress filled every pore of my body.

I knew that the phone would ring in a moment. It would be the security company asking me if everything was okay. They would want to know before they send the police. I'm thinking, *If I give them my password, then they'll know that it was a false alarm. If I don't give them the password, they'll send the*

police. The only problem is, how do I know if it's a false alarm? I'm
upstairs. Any intruder could be downstairs stealing my stuff. I don't
have video surveillance. I can creep downstairs to see if someone is
in my house. But if I do, and someone is in the house, I might get
shot. Isn't the whole point of having the security system so that the
police, not I, will ferret out any intruders? But on the other hand,
if some fluke has set off the alarm, I don't want police barging in the
house during the middle of the night.

Finally, I crept downstairs with a wingtip shoe as a weapon, only to find that, indeed, it was a false alarm.

If you don't have clear boundaries, then every time someone asks you to do something, an alarm goes off. There is no real predator. There is no theft actually taking place. You're asked a simple question. There should be a simple answer. All you have to do is say, "I don't have room for that in my schedule," or "I really can't take anything else on right now." But to you, it sounds the alarm because you feel like you *ought* to say yes, even though you don't want to say yes. It causes constant stress to your system.

When you do say yes just because you feel like you have to, it can lead to an even worse dynamic—resentment. You resent a person for asking you to do something because, being powerless to say no, the one who made the request is tantamount to a slave driver. I have often resented my wife asking me to do even simple chores because it has thrown me into a cycle of feeling like I ought to say yes, but not wanting to, and then feeling doomed either way. If I say yes, but didn't want to serve her at that time, then I resent doing the chore. If I say no, I feel like a bad husband for not always being there for her.

Either way, we both lose.

If I resent saying yes, then I develop a bitter root that "will spring up and defile many" (Hebrews 12:15). If I am ashamed for saying no, then I resent her putting me in the position of feeling bad about myself.

Of course, the problem is not hers. She is not seeking to make me the scapegoat or even the workhorse. She's just trying to manage a household and get some things done. At times, I've gotten mad and accused her of being overly demanding. Most of the time, she responds, "All I needed was a simple yes or no." In other words, she was simply communicating a need. There was something in *me* sounding the alarm—not *her*.

the plight of "the willing few"

Society exacerbates the scapegoat syndrome by applauding the person who is always available. We call on that person. You know the old adage. If you want something done, call a busy person to do it. Right? Call the guy, call the lady who never says no.

Society praises the driven people. We love the people who will take our problems upon themselves. We love the people who put a shoulder under our loads.

Never mind what happens to their families.

Never mind what happens to their souls.

Never mind that they work themselves into exhaustion.

We figuratively lay our hands on them, confess our problems over them, and send them out into the wilderness to carry our burdens away.

Sadly, there is no organization that applauds scapegoats louder than the church. We are confused because the Bible teaches us to turn the other cheek and, if someone asks you for your coat, give him your shirt as well. Martyrs are praised for bravely dying, and we know that it is more blessed to give than to receive.

Along with such biblical exhortations, we are faced with a mountain of need. We need someone to keep the nursery, someone to lead the youth, someone to mow the lawn, someone to visit the bereaved, and someone to serve on the committees. Desperate to get it all done, church leaders call on "the willing few." We applaud their hard work and lift them up as examples of good Christians who are doing what the Bible says to do.

While certain verses seem to encourage a boundary-less life, look at Jesus. Look at how sharply He defined Himself. He not only was known to dismiss a crowd in order to be alone (Mark 6:45), but on one occasion said to a dear friend: "Get behind me, Satan!" (8:33). After a leper was cleansed and told everyone about the healing, Jesus could no longer come into the towns, but instead had to stay outside in "lonely places" (1:40–45). Once, when a woman sneaked up, touched His garment, and received healing power, Jesus stopped, and insisted to speak to the woman in order to show that He was not a "force field" available for anyone to just "plug into" (5:31). Eventually, Jesus would lay down His life, but He made it clear "I lay down my life...no one takes it from me" (John 10:17–18).

How can you know the difference between a life of godly surrender and a life of unhealthy boundaries?

It's all in the motivation.

The scapegoat takes on more and more responsibility because he feels like he has to. The Spirit-filled person gives because of the leading of God and the overflow of love.

Does God call you to a life of complete surrender to Him? Absolutely. Does He want you to live a life of giving and service? Most certainly. But He never wants you to give out of compulsion or fear. He intends your ministry, like your life, to be an overflow of the abundance of love and joy He's deposited in you.

scapegoat redeemer

You don't have to be the scapegoat—Christ has already taken that role upon Himself.

As Jesus sweat blood in the Garden of Gethsemane, He saw the cup that He would drink. Like the vilest poison that was certain to kill, He knew it would be His death. Like the bitterest gall, it was sure to defile Him. In the cup of suffering that He would drink was not only the collective guilt of a sinful world, but also its shame.

The guilt of the rapist and the shame of the raped.

The guilt of the child molester and the shame of the molested.

In that cup would be the isolation and loneliness of a scapegoat, wandering in the demonic wilderness of hell itself.

He would be the first goat—bleeding to pay the debt. He would also be the second goat—carrying the sorrows of the world.

If you have taken a step to trust that Jesus' death has paid for your sins, then you know that it's a matter of faith. You acknowledge that you are completely bankrupt. You can't pay for your own sins, and trust that Jesus has done it for you. You let Him pay the price.

Letting Christ bear your shame is a step of faith, too.

You let Him be the scapegoat so that you won't have to. You come to Him honestly, admit your shame, and release it to Him in faith.

Choose wisely what "large items" you put on the curbside of your emotional life. Not only is it impossible for you to bear everyone's burdens—it isn't necessary! *Jesus already has*.

And please hear this: You don't have to be anybody's scapegoat.

Jesus was the Lamb and the Scapegoat.

ASK   A Question to Inquire:

Am I anyone's scapegoat? Am I making anyone my scapegoat?

BELIEVE   A Principle to Ponder:

"Most Christians I know have received the gift of Christ as payment for their sins but have not received the gift of Christ as the bearer of their shame. ...It explains why Christians, who are free from the law, are still trying to earn their way into the heaven they have already been promised. It explains why a person can be a born-again, bound-for-eternal-glory child of

God and be meaner than a junkyard dog. And it explains why we put too much of our 'large items' on the curbside of life."

Christ died to take my sin and my shame.

I can help others change by praying, sowing good seed, practicing blessing, and treating people as if they're owners.

CHOOSE   A Commitment to Keep:

I choose today to examine what I've put at the curbside of my life for "large item pickup." I am committed to being no one's scapegoat because only Christ can carry anyone's burdens away.

pray

O God, I want to make no one my scapegoat and I want to be a scapegoat to no one. You alone are able to carry away our sorrows, burdens, and pain. Thank You for bearing not only my sin, but also my shame. Show me the ways I've made scapegoats of others so I can change. Show me the ways that I have served as scapegoat for others, so I can come out of the wilderness and into the light. I release my sin and shame to You, Lord, through Christ, AMEN.

CHAPTER EIGHT

THE AGONY
OF VICTORY

Years after North Carolina's 1982 NCAA national championship victory, I was thumbing through a UNC basketball pictorial history. Although he never had the privilege of meeting me, Michael Jordan and I were classmates! I was a UNC student during the 1982 championship season. So, when I came to that section of the pictorial, I paused to relive the moments. There was Michael Jordan's game-winning shot over Georgetown. There was the team celebrating, cutting down the net. It brought back memories as I smiled upon those pages.

Then, a strange photo stopped me.

The black and white photograph must have been snapped moments after the team exited the floor. Unclear whether a locker room or a hallway, the backdrop was an inglorious cinder block wall. Clearly, the game had been played and won. The basketball net, garland-like, hung around James Worthy's neck as a testimonial to the victory. The dream had been realized.

The battle was finished. The adulation had begun. But for that odd moment, the camera had captured James Worthy and Sam Perkins not celebrating—in fact, not even smiling. Instead, the basketball players looked spent, emotionless and drained. Almost sad.

Surely, moments after that strange photo was captured, the team surged back onto the floor. Worthy would arrive to receive his MVP award and the team would appear to wave once again to the applause of the auditorium. But what kind of odd moment had I witnessed through the camera's report? It was a moment of sober reality in the midst of a great accomplishment. Unlike Wide World of Sports' famous claim to share the "thrill of victory and the agony of defeat," I had found a photo depicting the "agony of victory."

HOLLOW TRIUMPH

One might think that the solution to shame's taunts is victory. Succeed enough and it will silence the shaming voice that has haunted you for so long. I once thought that the answer to my esteem was to win a grand enough victory, realize a great enough dream, and all self-doubt would be eclipsed.

It would certainly seem that our shame should be swallowed up in the wake of the grandeur of our accomplishments. I'm tempted to think that lasting joy will come when the net I have so coveted is finally upon my neck.

But somehow, strangely, it isn't enough.

Have you ever found a victory great enough to dissolve your anxieties? Have you ever accomplished something so profound that you were not tempted with the same nagging discontent in your soul?

In reality, even our best moments are tainted with the taunts of shame. Bring home all A's and one B, and someone will ask you about the cause for the B. Preach a sermon that touches hundreds but receive one disparaging note. Which do you remember most—the hundreds of grateful handshakes or the one accusatory letter? Become a finalist in the beauty contest and discover one tiny blemish that consumes your thoughts as you step into the lights. Win your tenth professional golf tournament and ready yourself for the question, "But why can't you win a major?" Finally buy the house of your dreams and then find yourself wondering if the weeds in your yard are a blot upon the neighborhood. Be awarded the promotion you've worked so hard to get and then spend a restless night wondering if you really deserved it.

Shame is no respecter of persons. Shame lies in the gutter with you after your worst failures, *Look at you, you failure; can't you do anything right?* But shame also escorts you down victory lane, *Sure, you've won, but so what? It's still not enough. It's still not perfect. And what about next time—what if you lose next time?*

There is a unique vulnerability in our seasons of accomplishment. I find my greatest temptation to despair is Monday morning after a glorious Sunday. Adam and Eve's temptation came amidst the glory of Paradise. Israel's cowardice to conquer Canaan came on the heels of a glorious Passover provision and a parted sea. David's rooftop lust for Bathsheba came after he had built the borders, bolstered the economy, and won the praise of all the people. Jesus' wilderness temptation followed His dove-descending baptism and launch of His public ministry.

And then there was Elijah.

snatching defeat from the jaws of victory

Into the midst of a pluralistic, pagan society, this miracle working man mysteriously appears. In contrast to the many forms of worship unto the many gods of Canaan, Elijah's name means literally "The LORD is my God." He is one of the greatest heroes in the history of Israel. He has such prophetic anointing that, by his mouth, there is famine or there is rain. He was fed by ravens, brought a boy back to life, and was heralded: "You are a man of God and…the word of the LORD from your mouth is true" (1 Kings 17:24).

On a divine commission, Elijah moves resolutely to meet King Ahab and tell him that the Lord plans to send rain. Ahab greets the man of God with a shaming taunt: "Is that you, you troubler of Israel?" The confident Elijah is neither deterred nor distracted by Ahab's disdain.

Instead, the seemingly unflappable prophet issues the command: "Now summon the people from all over Israel to meet me on Mount Carmel. And bring the four hundred and fifty prophets of Baal and the four hundred prophets of Asherah…" (1 Kings 18:19). Elijah declares a challenge: "Get two bulls for us. Let them choose one for themselves, and let them cut it into pieces and put it on the wood but not set fire to it. I will prepare the other bull and put it on the wood but not set fire to it. Then you call on the name of your god, and I will call upon the name of the LORD. The god who answers by fire—he is God" (vv. 23–24).

The Baalian prophets cry, dance, writhe in the dust, and cut their own flesh, but the bull's blood just pools in the dust beneath their barren altar.

When it's the man of God's turn, Elijah prays with power: "Answer me, O LORD, answer me, so these people will know that you, O LORD, are God..." (v. 37).

Then the fire falls, licking up the blood and the water and prostrating the people who are compelled to cry, "The LORD—he is God! The LORD—he is God!" (v. 39). Elijah's command to destroy the pagan prophets is consistent with Jehovah's command and accentuates the comprehensive quality of this victory.

What victory could be greater? It was a triumph against all odds. There's nothing sweeter than an underdog victory that proves the underdog to be worthy after all. It's the ultimate, "I told you so." And the Lord's conquest over Baal was supremely public. It was no hanging-chad-subject-to-question victory. It was a landslide. A cosmic mandate. It's hard to imagine a more unlikely, more public, or more comprehensive victory than Elijah's triumph at Mount Carmel.

So how do you explain what happened next?

After a display like Mount Carmel, surely Ahab would repent, rise up, call the prophet blessed and say, like the widow of the resurrected son, "Now I know that you are a man of God and that the word of the LORD from your mouth is the truth."

But it wasn't to be. Instead of repenting, the evil king

scuttles back to his castle and whimpers to his woman. Showing himself to be more mouse than man, Ahab "told Jezebel everything Elijah had done..." (1 Kings 19:1). Instead of falling to his knees in wonder, the weak king whines to his pagan consort until she takes up the banner of persecution in his behalf: "May the gods deal with me, be it ever so severely, if by this time tomorrow I do not make [Elijah's] life like that of one of [the Baal prophets]" (v. 2).

You may have your moments of miraculous accomplishment. You may stand on the platform with the Olympic gold upon your neck. You may become the president of your kindergarten class, the president of the PTA, or the president of the United States. You may win the lottery, win the hand of your beloved, or win the admiration of a whole society. But this side of heaven, there will never be a season so sweet, nor a platform so high that you will be exempt from the attack of the enemy.

There will always be a Jezebel.

She may be quiet for a while, she may be waiting in the wings, but count on it...she's there. As long as the devil is permitted to roam the earth, there will be a voice of shame that follows you even up to the pinnacles of your performance, even up to the highest levels of kingdom service.

As we read the drama for the first time, we find no suspense in Jezebel's threat. Hey, this is *Elijah* she's talking about. You don't mess with a guy who could pray drought to cover the land and fire to fall from the sky. What was she thinking? It would be like an ant threatening an elephant...wouldn't it? One pagan woman threatening the man of God who defeated 450 of Baal's best?

And yet what do we read?

"Elijah was afraid and ran for his life" (v. 3).

when your best isn't good enough

What has bewitched our hero?

"Elijah," we want to shout, "it's just one woman. Forget her—she's a flea. Let her bluster. Dismiss her threat. You've raised the dead. You've felt the fire of God on your face. Relax, man of God—how could *you* be afraid?!"

But Elijah has no energy to face another opponent. And in the agony of victory, he runs pell-mell into a shame-filled depression in the desert. He does what the deeply depressed do, ponders the benefits of death—an escape from the shame of life. "I have had enough LORD.... Take my life; I am no better than my ancestors" (v. 4). The depressed winner crawls under the dubious shade of a desert broom tree, and he falls into slumber with the dark hope of never waking up.

The prophet whose prayer life the apostle James commemorates as the model for our own faith, does not pray. The man who boldly interceded, "Answer me, O LORD," now imagines God has no answers. The man who lived according to the word of God is suddenly living according to the word of Jezebel.

In his exhaustion and false expectations of a respite after Carmel, Elijah makes a tragic mistake. Instead of going to God with his anxiety, releasing his shame, and finding courage in the Lord to face his adversary, Elijah tries to bear it himself in isolation.

In author Gordon Dalbey's words: "The effort to hide the truth of your inadequacy and bear your shame consumes you and sabotages your destiny. When all your energies focus on an enemy, you have no energy or vision left to discern and fulfill your calling in life. The enemy thereby begins to define you. Hell, therefore, could aptly be described as 'trying to bear your own shame.' It's living a lie, forever sandbagging against the rising tide of truth—an eternally exhausting distraction from your holy destiny."[11]

Elijah, from his heavenly experience on Mount Carmel, finds himself in the hell of trying to bear his own shame.

Imagine for a moment the prophet's mental torment. *You gave it your best, but your best wasn't good enough. You gave it your all, but your all didn't measure up. If you tried that hard and failed, you might as well give up. Besides, you're the only one left— no one notices; there's no one to help you. In the end, you're no better than those who have gone before you. You're like everyone else—a failure.*

If you have tried something only halfheartedly and you fail, it's different. Then you can say, *Well, I didn't really give it my all; I'll just try harder.* But our Mount Carmels are opportune moments for the enemy because those are the seasons in which we *have* given it our all. We *have* done our best. The pain is finding your best not to be enough.

Elijah's plea for death is a plea for escape from the pressure of life. For Elijah, that day, sleep would be his anesthesia. Food, alcohol, pornography, busyness, materialism—almost anything can serve as your plea for escape. Suicide is simply the final attempt to find an anesthesia that will turn off the pain of life's pressures. But suicide is just the move from one hell to another, our anesthetics always wear off, and our Jezebels still chase us down.

As with Paul's urgent prayer for the removal of a painful thorn in the flesh, we long for an escape from the last critical voice in our lives. In our pain, we seek relief from the demonic messengers who taunt us, and we want to believe that if we could just be rid of that final shaming voice, then we could live in peace. Then, we imagine, when there are no more Jezebels, we will finally find some joy.

Stop here, friend, and let the following words sink in...and be set free. There is no accomplishment great enough to obliterate the pressures of life. There is no level of success high enough to exempt you from Jezebel. Never be tempted to excuse yourself from the battle. Never, while you live in this broken world, imagine there will be a day when you can safely shed your spiritual armor and declare the war to be over.

It's just not so.

No matter what level of spiritual maturity you might attain, the enemy of your soul will fight and contend with you until your last breath.

Why should you find that encouraging?

Because once you realize that the battle will never be won in this life, once you realize that you will always be in process, yet never achieve perfection, then you'll be ready for the Jezebels. You won't be surprised when shame comes at you from unexpected directions.

Let's face it, you will never, never prove yourself to everybody.

You will always be substandard in somebody's eyes. There will always be people ready to criticize, critique, and demean you. It comes with the territory. It's as predictable as rain in April and mosquitoes in July.

So don't let it throw you.

Don't let it deflate your joy.

Don't let it pull the rug out from under your peace.

You might as well be set free from the bondage of performance. God would eventually deal with Jezebel as He had dealt with the prophets of Baal. And God will eventually deal with all the voices that shame you, too. God will eventually silence Satan himself. But today, God's answer for your shame is not your personal success nor God's pledge to remove your thorn. God's answer is, as it has always been, to be with you in your pain, to bear your shame, and nourish you for the journey ahead.

God will not leave His children comfortless. When you give up on yourself, God doesn't. What does God do after Mount Carmel? Does He send a bully to beat up Elijah and rattle some sense into his shame-filled head?

Not at all.

In fact, He sends an angel.

"get up and eat"

First, the angel touches the prophet. Never underestimate the power of touch! Elijah had left his servant behind and went off into the desert alone. Feeling ashamed and defeated, he thought solitude was what he needed most. In reality, it's what an ashamed person needs least.

What he really needed was a touch.

And that's just what God provided. We needn't be surprised. After all, this is the God who walked with Adam and Eve in the cool of the Garden. This is the God who became flesh and pitched His tent with us. This is the God who said, "Abide in Me and I will abide in you." This is the God who touched lepers and unclean women. When we have no desire for company or even feel worthy of it, God comes near. When we settle for sinful distraction, God knocks at our heart's door and asks for intimacy.

I find this angelic encounter somewhat surprising. The courier from heaven didn't crawl under the broom tree with Elijah to join his pity party.

Instead, the angel's words were a command from God.

"Get up and eat."

It wasn't a suggestion. It wasn't a prescription he could fill at his leisure. It was a command. There is nothing more precious than a personal command from God. Inherent in every command from God is a promise from God. The grass might wither, flowers might fade, and prophets might grow depressed, but the word of the Lord will not fail. If He commands me to eat, then it must be that I will be nourished. And if He wants me nourished, there must be something left for me to do.

Get up and eat.

The glory of Mount Carmel did not excuse Elijah from the human need for daily bread. Mountaintop moments never replace daily meals. Are you weak? Get up and eat. Are you ashamed? Get up and eat. Are you hopeless? Get up and eat. Feast upon His grace. Feed upon His Word. Eat the bread of life.

The angel continues, "...for the journey is too much for you." Too much for *you*—but not too much for God. The pressure of life is too much for you—but not too much for God. Jezebel is too much for you—but not too much for God. The shame of the past is too much for you—but not too much for God. "Cast all your burdens upon Him because He cares for you," Scripture tells us. Don't try to bear the unbearable, because "the battle is the LORD'S." And yes, you will win, but it will be "Not by might, nor by power, but by my Spirit" (1 Peter 5:7; 1 Samuel 17:47; Zechariah 4:6).

What is the good news to Elijah that propels him forward from his shame? It's a little ironic. God says to the victorious prophet who thinks he's done it all, "You have a great journey still ahead."

Life is a journey, not a destination. Shame-based saints tend to focus on arriving at a point of success to prove themselves. Grace-filled saints focus on walking with God.

To say, "You have a long way still to go" is to say, "There is more life to be lived." It is to say, "The best is yet to come." Elijah had a destiny still to fulfill. Elijah's mantle would be placed on Elisha. His anointing would double. He would ascend in a whirlwind. He would shimmer next to Jesus, talking to Him on the Mount of Transfiguration. So, get up, Elijah, you've won a great victory, but there's still a wonderful journey ahead. And as poet Robert Frost might say it, "Miles to go before you sleep."

Savor your successes, but don't idolize them. Your victories cannot be your gods. Your awards will never be your answers. No number of NCAA championship nets will soothe the shame in your soul.

Win for the fun of the game, for the glory of God, and for the fact that the Spirit of victory lives inside of you. But be free, I say to every Elijah. Your prize never has been, and never will be, dependent upon your perfection. The real prize is not a pinnacle. It's a Person.

Get up and eat.

Take God's hand.

The journey ahead is greater than you know.

ASK   A Question to Inquire:

When have I succeeded but felt empty?

BELIEVE   A Principle to Ponder:

"You may become the president of your kindergarten class, the president of the PTA or the president of the United States.... But this side of heaven, there will never be a season so sweet, nor a platform so high that you will be exempt from the attack of the enemy."

The secret to my healing is not more achievement or success. The secret to my healing is knowing that I can be nourished today for an even greater journey tomorrow.

CHOOSE   A Commitment to Keep:

I choose today to get up from my place of shame, take God's nourishment, and set my eyes on the glorious journey that is still ahead.

pray

Lord, despite the triumphs of my life, You know I am prone to discouragement when the enemy keeps attacking. Send Your angels to pick me up, speak Your Word to lift me up and show me the journey that is still ahead. I thank You for all that You have done in my life—for every victory and every accomplishment. But Lord, don't let my successes lull me into spiritual vulnerability. Gird me with Your full armor and grant me the faith to see that the best is yet to come. In Jesus' name, AMEN.

how to get
people to change

I'm guessing you're not overly fond of this chapter title. It might make you wince, just a little.

It might confuse you, just a bit.

I thought I was learning to accept other people, not change them.

We've all been manipulated by high-control people and, when you finally start getting the shame off you, the last thing you want is someone trying to change you. Right?

I have brown eyes. I sure don't need my wife telling me she would rather I have blue eyes. I want to say "Take me or leave me, baby, but I'm a brown-eyed boy." I'm sure I've told engaged couples, "Don't enter into marriage wanting to change the other person." I'm sure I've implied it a thousand times in sermons over the years, "Don't go around trying to get people to change."

I was wrong.

What a ridiculous conclusion for a preacher to make! *Don't go around trying to get people to change?* Isn't that what I do every day of my life? Isn't that the whole reason I'm called into ministry—to try to get people to change from a life of darkness to a life of light? Isn't that why I'm writing this book—because I want people to change?

If I'm honest, I must admit that my whole life is devoted to "going around trying to get people to change." In fact, now that I'm being honest about it, I want almost everybody around me to change.

I want my wife to have no worries.

I want my kids to grow up more every day.

I want my church members to love God more, love other people more, and give more money to the work of the kingdom.

I don't even know you, but I want you to change, too. I'd like you to be less motivated by shame and more motivated by the love of God. I'd like for you to love your spouse more deeply and serve God more joyfully.

Of course I want people to change, don't you? I don't care how spiritual you are, you can't tell me there isn't something about your spouse or your children or your employees or your neighbors that you would like to change. Even people who are very accepting want others to become more accepting!

Moses wanted the Hebrew people to change—to quit being so stiff-necked and quit dancing around golden calves. Joshua wanted them to change—to have more courage and to take the land. The prophets wanted the people to change, to turn away from idolatry and worship God alone and to show justice to the oppressed. The apostle Paul wanted his congregations to change. "Be transformed by the renewing of your mind" (Romans 12:2).

Jesus' purpose in the world was to change lives. It's why He touched lepers, lifted up prostitutes, and poured His time and energy into the twelve disciples. He told people to follow Him so that their lives would change. His message was "Repent, for the kingdom of heaven is at hand" (Matthew 4:17, NKJV). Repent, literally "change your mind," was the word Jesus put on the disciples' lips as He sent them out to preach. His final commission to us was for us to go into all the world and get people to change.

Of course we want people to change. It's why teachers teach, parents parent, and salesmen sell. We want people to know something, do something, or have something better than what they have now.

Granted, our desire for others to change can spawn an array of sins. For example, it's no sin to want your wife to have a better figure, but it's a hellish sin called coveting if you wish she looked like your best friend's wife. And you become an accomplice of Satan if you condemn her or disdain her. There's no sin in wanting your husband to get promoted at work, but if you want it so that you'll feel more secure, it has become a sin called idolatry. Then, if you nag him about the promotion, you become an ally of hell for the purposes of eroding his confidence.

There's no sin in wanting people to change.

The sin comes when we try to motivate them in the wrong way.

STRATEGIES FOR CHANGE

There's no sin in wanting your husband to talk to you more, but it's wrong and unproductive to nag him about it. There's no sin in wanting your daughter to clean her room, but it's wrong and unproductive to tell her she's a bad kid who'll probably make someone a miserable wife some day.

We need to quit trying to convince ourselves that it's wrong to want other people to change and start focusing on *how* we can help them change in a biblical way.

Clearly, the best thing we can do is pray. Intercede for those who need to change. Ask God to open the eyes of their hearts. Stand in the gap. Envision God's best for them. Plead the promises of God over their lives. Pray the Scriptures over them. Ask for the Holy Spirit to convict them. Pray for God to put godly influences in their lives. Pray.

In addition to praying, I've concluded that there are three basic, biblical strategies to help others change.

1. We change a negative spirit by sowing the opposite spirit.

There is an inviolable law at work in the visible and invisible world called sowing and reaping. Whatever a person sows, that he or she also reaps. Acorns never produce palm trees, only oaks. Apple seeds never produce orange trees, only apple trees.

If you have a yard with weeds, you'll never get rid of the weeds by sowing more weeds. So why do we think that we're going to get our friends to be more kind to us by giving them the silent treatment? Why do we think we're going to get our enemies to stop telling half-truths about us by telling half-truths about them? Why do we think that we're going to get our children to respect us more by disrespecting them?

Paul spells the principle out: "Do not be overcome by evil,

but overcome evil with good" (Romans 12:21). Jesus' life and sacrifice was the ultimate demonstration of this universal principle. In order to bring about change in those who hated Him, He sowed love. In order to make people more forgiving, He forgave them.

You might as well settle it in your thinking right now. You cannot influence anyone to repent from evil by inflicting evil. In fact, if there is a negative attitude or behavior that you want someone to change, you must sow the opposite—a godly attitude or behavior. Do you want someone to stop judging you? Then don't judge yourself. Do you want to be forgiven? Then forgive. In fact, knowing how to help a person change is as easy as the familiar words from the Sermon on the Mount: "Do to others as you would have them do to you" (Luke 6:31).

You can't heal shame by shaming someone. You can't cast out or rebuke someone else's shame-based fear. "Perfect love casts out fear" (1 John 4:18, NKJV). The orphan spirit cannot be yanked out of a person, it must be displaced in a person. If a person is going to quit acting so insecurely, their insecurity must be displaced by continued acceptance.

If a woman is going to quit overeating, it is more likely to come through her husband's love than in response to his rebuke. It's not the husband's scorn, "I'm ashamed of your overweight figure," that will help his wife change. Rather, it is making the wife more at home in his love that will displace the need in the woman to seek comfort from food.

It's not the wife's disdain at her husband's workaholism— "You ought to be ashamed of how little time you spend at home with me and the kids"—that will motivate him to change. The ashamed husband will feel worse about his inadequacy and will avoid home all the more because it accentuates those feelings. Instead, the wife of a workaholic does better to treat the husband with God-given grace and, when she does speak of the problem, convey how much she loves being with her husband rather than how disgusted and disappointed she is to have an inattentive husband.

2. We enable positive change through the power of blessing.

God blessed Adam and Eve and *then* told them to be fruitful and multiply. The blessing came first. The first couple's commission to take dominion of the earth grew out of the prophetic blessing and affirmation of their value and strength as creatures made in the image of God.

When Isaac inadvertently blessed the conniving younger brother, Jacob, instead of the older Esau who was supposed to receive the blessing, Isaac couldn't undo it.

For years, I read that story and thought, *What's the big deal here? Why doesn't Isaac just say, "whoops, made a mistake," and redo the blessing for the proper son?* Instead, Isaac trembled and said to the grieving Esau, "I have blessed [your brother]—and indeed, he will be blessed" (Genesis 27:33). The blessing was so powerful to the patriarch that he understood it to be irrevocable, and a guarantee of life change for the one blessed.

Other than God's Spirit Himself, the power of blessing is the single greatest force for change in the universe. More than positive reinforcement or helpful affirmation, biblical blessing has a prophetic power to release positive change in a person.

Conversely, curse has negative power and, if unrenounced, can shape our lives for the worse.

Nothing has helped me more in parenting than comprehending the power of blessing. If I see my children acting impatiently or unkindly toward others, I know that they're feeling unblessed. If I see them act loving and caring, I know that it's because their "love tank" is full and overflowing.

Often at the dinner table, I will take a moment, like Hebrew patriarchs of old, and bless my wife and children personally. It might be as simple as telling Abigail that I saw her do something sweet that day and proclaim to her that she is a sweet child. It was so delightful when she was small to watch her reaction to her father's blessing. Lacking any ability to hide how delighted she was, she would often just blurt out to my wife a recapitulation of my words. If I told her she was smart, she'd look at my wife and exclaim, "Daddy says Abby is smart!"

On one occasion at the dinner table, I told her, "Abby, you have beautiful eyes." As was usual, she turned and made an exclamation to her mother, but this time it was different: "Mommy, I love you more than the whole wide world!" Her father's blessing directly empowered her to love her mother more!

We discipline our children, but bless them as we do. If I have to spank or take away a privilege, I try to accompany it with a blessing: "Bennett, you are not a mean child; you are kind, and I know that you're going to be a blessing to many people throughout your life. That's why I can't allow you to treat your sister unkindly." In other words, we seek to discipline the children for acting contrary to a positive destiny. Instead of shaming them, isolating them, or cursing them, we affirm them even in discipline.

Why do we think that we are going to bring about a state of blessedness in someone by cursing the person? How foolish to think that we will give a person courage by calling him a coward! How absurd to think that we will make a student brighter by calling her stupid!

If you want someone to change, envision a positive future over that individual. Find an effective way to communicate your positive picture to him or her. Don't give up or revert to cursing if you don't see immediate results. Seeds take time to grow. You might get a more immediate reaction by cursing and shaming, but such tactics will, in the end, make a person's behavior worsen. Bless, do not curse, and you will help people change.

3. We help people embrace responsibility by treating them as if they're owners, not slaves.

When Bennett was six, we sat on the front steps to sip lemonade on our day of play when my boy startled me with a question out of the blue: "Dad, what's a slave?"

I wondered where he'd even heard of slavery and wasn't prepared to educate him about the sins of society just yet. But I swallowed hard and tried to give a simple answer.

"Well, Bennett, a slave is a person who belongs to another person, called a master, and the slave has to do whatever that master says to do. The people of God were slaves once during Moses' time. And sadly, in the early days of our own country, people had slaves. It makes me sad, Bennett, to think of it—but it's part of our past."

Bennett was quiet and reflective for a few moments.

"Dad?"

"Yes, Bennett?"

"I belong to *you*, and I have to do everything you say, don't I?"

I gulped. "Well, uh, yeah, you do belong to me and, er, yes, I expect you to obey me. But it's so different. You're my son, not my slave."

"What's the difference?"

"Well, Bennett, you must understand that if a slave doesn't do everything the master says, then the slave might get beaten."

"Dad?"

Oh no. I saw it coming. "Yes, Bennett?"

"If I don't do what you say do, sometimes you spank me, don't you?"

"Well, yes, I do sometimes spank you, but it's different."

I succeeded in changing the subject and moving on. But *I* couldn't move on. I was left to meditate for days on his question. What's the difference between a slave and a son?

I settled on some clear distinctions. Slaves are valued for their productivity, whereas sons are valued for their position. Though I might ask Bennett to do some simple chores, the fact is, of course, that I give far more to Bennett than he gives to me.

When Dudley Hall's son was about nine years old, Dudley confronted the boy about procrastinating in doing some yard work. Finally, Dudley picked up the paddle and David took off. When the father finally caught up to his son, he could hardly believe what the nine-year-old claimed: "The only reason you had me was so I could work for you." Dudley dropped the paddle and fell to the ground laughing as he began calculating the natal hospital bills, the dental bills, the clothing expenses, and nine years of food costs. His conclusion? "I had been ripped off! I had spent at least thirty thousand dollars to get my lawn mowed a few times!"[12]

I also came to recognize that slaves live primarily by rules whereas sons live by relationship. I saw that, fundamentally, slaves live trying to avoid pain whereas true sons get ahead by claiming promises. I knew that although my children might try to avoid punishment, they spend the majority of their energy reminding me of the promises I've made. "But, Dad, you *promised* we were going to get ice cream." I find it nearly impossible to break a promise that is shoved back into my face repeatedly.

My meditation enabled me to learn enough distinctions to answer Bennett's question, but I had a sense that I hadn't uncovered the full answer. Something fundamental was still missing from my understanding. I was still left with the basic question of what motivates us to work hard in life. How does a father motivate a son differently than the way a master motivates a slave? More straightforwardly, how can we challenge our children, supervise our employees, and exhort loved ones without shaming them?

Most invitations to responsibility that I've heard have been basically shaming. Preachers want their parishioners to act like good Christians. Most preachers don't want to shame their listeners, so they tell them God loves them and speak about being saved by God's grace. But whenever they start talking about how important it is to live a moral life, to serve in the nursery, help at the church work day, or give to the financial campaign, they don't know how to issue the challenge without saying, in essence, "You ought to do more and you ought to be ashamed of yourself if you don't."

For most of my fifteen years of preaching, I solved the dilemma by simply avoiding it. I had no idea how to motivate people to growth without shaming them about their lack of maturity. I almost never taught about stewardship, and when I did, I sort of apologized before I did, got it over as quickly as possible, and then wondered why the church's financial picture wasn't getting better. I never spoke about repentance, either. It just seemed harsh. I just spoke about what I knew was good—the sweet grace of God, and the invitation we have to receive the love of God.

I knew something was missing from my preaching. And I truly wanted people to take responsibilities and act more maturely. But I had no idea how to do it. How can we get people to grow up and act responsibly without manipulating or scolding them?

Then, one day, it happened. The veil lifted. I saw the answer in all its glory. It was suddenly so plain. So simple. A simple revelation that would change my thinking, preaching, and parenting forever.

THE REVELATION

Mickey, our church's executive director, has one of the deepest work ethics of any man I know. On this particular occasion, he was at the church on a Saturday afternoon performing a task that should have been done that week by someone else.

"What are you doing up here on a Saturday afternoon?" I asked him. "You know that isn't your job."

Mickey shrugged. "Well, it needs to be done."

"Yes, I know that. But why didn't the other person do it?"

"I guess it's just a matter of ownership," Mickey responded. And then he added, "I wish our volunteers and staff could understand that we aren't trying to kill them, we're trying to set them free."

And that was the moment when the veil lifted.

I heard the words echoing deep in my heart and knew it to be the word of the Lord. One short phrase of revelation changed my thinking and my preaching forever: *Only free people own things.*

That's the difference between slaves and heirs! Slaves don't own the farm on which they labor. The free man, who owns the estate, works hard because it is *his*. The slave works only up to the point necessary to avoid punishment. When the master says, "Okay, you can quit plowing the field now," the slave quits. Of course. It wouldn't enter the slave's mind to think, *Well, maybe I'll keep working a bit more and finish out this row.*

But the owner of the farm, on the other hand, deeply cares about his land. From his point of view, work isn't an obligation, it's an investment. He might look at the sky and say to himself, *With the rain coming tomorrow, I think I'll work late into the evening tonight. I really need to finish the plowing if I'm going to get the crop planted on time.*

People who shame their children, employees, or parishioners eventually produce slaves. We can get people to work more, try harder, and perform better by threatening the withdrawal of our love and acceptance, but we will never set them free. We produce workers who have no joy and who are looking for a way to escape the responsibilities that so haunt their consciences. Once we have been filled with shame it produces slave thinking. *I have to perform in order to be accepted. Therefore, I'll work hard, but only up to the point necessary to avoid rejection.*

We find ourselves studying to make A's, not to improve our minds. We will work for the promotion, the new title, or the better salary, but not for the improvement of the business. In our shame, we don't look at life like owners who are investing ourselves in a great dream, but more like slaves trying to escape further hurt.

Only free people own things. The key to motivating people to work hard is not shaming them like slaves. The key to motivating people is to liberate them. Only inasmuch as people see themselves as owners will they take responsibility.

Often a mature Christian wife will want her husband to be more of a spiritual leader in the home. In her frustration, she will shame the husband. "Why can't you be a better husband and father by leading us in family prayer, devotionals, and church attendance?"

The husband might respond dutifully as a slave, or, more likely, retreat to his ball game on TV to avoid the shame. Usually, while shaming the husband for his passivity, the wife becomes all the more domineering. The man is more likely to respond to a wife who invites his leadership through submission. The wise wife knows that she must show increasing levels of trust in her husband's parental input in order for the husband to come out of his cave of passivity. The husband of a domineering wife remains passive because he feels no ownership of the decision making in the household or in the parenting of the children.

Conversely, a husband who wants his wife to show him more affection, comfort, and physical intimacy, often shames the wife out of his frustration: "You're not a good wife—if you want to be a better partner, you'll have sex with me more often." As a result, the wife will either dutifully participate in lovemaking more often to avoid the shame, or she will find herself feeling increasingly less attracted to her husband. So what has the husband accomplished? He's produced a slave who responds to him out of fear of abandonment rather than genuine attraction.

I have known wise husbands, however, who dared to share their weaknesses with their wives in order to build an open relationship. As the husband opens his soul to share the empty places, the woman is irresistibly drawn in as a comforter. Likewise, the wise husband who longs for more lovemaking, conveys to his wife not the threat of abandonment, but his exclusive commitment to her. By declaring, "I will never leave you," the husband invests himself more deeply toward his wife and, in so doing, helps her invest herself more deeply unto him. The more she is appreciated as his exclusive choice among women in the world, the more she will want to give herself to him—not with the duty of a slave, but with the joy of an heir of life together. It is her sense of full partnership, and his mutual submission, that attracts her emotionally and physically to her husband.

OWNERSHIP AND MOTIVATION

Mickey and I felt the glory of God upon us as we shared insights back and forth that day in the church office. We were laughing and high-fiving each other and exclaiming, "I see it! I see it!"

The Hebrews' hope of ownership of the Promised Land would be the fuel to make them fight. The Passover narrative describes a real people on their journey to a real land. But it was a shadow of something even more real to come. Just as the whole Old Testament story turns on the question of who owns the land, the New Covenant gospel is a story of an invisible land called the kingdom of God. By the blood of the true Passover Lamb, we are brought from the land of bondage under the law into the glorious liberty of God's grace. We who once labored under the threat of punishment are escorted into a glorious inheritance and given the startling news that we have been blessed with every spiritual blessing in Christ (Ephesians 1).

This transforming deliverance was the joy of the apostle Paul's life and the substance of his preaching: "For you did not receive a spirit that makes you a slave again to fear, but you received the Spirit of sonship. And by him we cry, 'Abba, Father.' The Spirit himself testifies with our spirit that we are God's children. Now if we are children, then we are heirs— heirs of God and coheirs with Christ..." (Romans 8:15–17). As owners, then, in the kingdom of God, we are called "more than conquerors" (v. 37) and told that we now reign with Christ (5:17).

I don't pick up trash out of your yard, but I pick it up in my yard. I don't wash your car, I wash my car. I don't clean your gutters, I clean my gutters (well, one time I did). Why? Because I don't own your yard, your car, or your gutters. We work to care for, improve, and protect what we own.

As Mickey and I danced about the office under the joyful anointing of this revelation, my mind danced to Scriptures that I had not previously comprehended. I especially turned to the enigmatic words of Paul to the Galatians: "What I am saying is that as long as the heir is a child, he is no different from a slave, although he owns the whole estate. He is subject to guardians and trustees until the time set by his father. So also, when we were children, we were in slavery under the basic principles of the world. But...you are no longer a slave, but a son; and since you are a son, God has made you also an heir" (Galatians 4:1–7).

My children are heirs, but until they take ownership of their lives, they are no different than slaves. When I tell my boy he has to eat his green beans, he asks me, "How many beans do I have to eat?" When I tell my little girl that she has to clean her room, she comes back every few minutes and says, "Have I cleaned enough?" In other words, "Tell me, Master, when I can stop without fear of punishment."

One day, I hope and pray, my boy will eat fruits and vegetables for his own sake, rather than because I tell him to. He will take ownership of his body, and as the possessor of such an incredibly valuable thing, he will want to feed it healthy food so that it will last a long time. One day, I hope, for the sake of her future husband, my Abigail will clean her room not because she has to, but because she has come to realize that it's her room. And because it is *hers*, she values it and wants it to be orderly and usable.

In other words, as a parent I have the responsibility to tell the children what they must do. But I have a bigger goal in mind—helping them grow up into an inheritance. My short-term need is to give them rules, but my long-term goal is for them to live, not under the fear of the law, but under the joy of ownership.

If I had a million dollars to give my children, I sure wouldn't give it to them now. I definitely wouldn't give it to them when they turn sixteen, either. We can only be entrusted with an inheritance when we have taken ownership of life. My ultimate goal in parenting, therefore, is to help my children grow up so that they can one day receive their full inheritance.

If we want others to change, we must find ways to do more than issue laws. We must find ways to treat them like owners so that they will discover that responsibilities are privileges. If you feel like your job is a drag, ask an unemployed man if he thinks a job is a chore or a privilege. If you think that exercise is a laborious yoke, ask a paralytic if she views walking on the treadmill as an inconvenience or a privilege.

Only free people own things. Therefore, treat people in liberating ways. Escort people into freedom. Treat them like owners.

CHOOSE YOUR RESULTS

Face it. You want people to change. That's okay. God wants them to change, too. But none of us own magic wands. There will be no "poof," and presto, you have a new husband or wife or child or friend. In our impatience, we try to find a shortcut called shame or guilt. It works temporarily. People fear our rejection and so they'll try harder to be what we want them to be.

The fruit of shame, however, is slavery.

If you make slaves of others around you, they'll eventually want to break free from you. If you choose the way of God— you'll produce free people. You can't control and manipulate free people. But free people are invested in life and, therefore, want to get better. If you want to produce slaves, shame people. You will have accomplished the goal of hell. If you want to produce free people, treat them as such. You'll have accomplished the goal of heaven. I've tried both ways.

I recommend heaven's way. It works a lot better.

ASK   A Question to Inquire:

Who have I been trying to change? Am I doing it God's way or the enemy's way?

BELIEVE   A Principle to Ponder:

"We need to quit trying to convince ourselves that it's wrong to want other people to change and start focusing on *how* we can help others change in a biblical way. We need to start asking: "What is the right way to motivate, empower, and spur people toward the changes we know would be good for them and for those they touch?"

I can help others change by praying, sowing good seed, practicing blessing, and treating people as if they're owners.

CHOOSE   A Commitment to Keep:

I choose today to abandon the unhealthy ways that I try to change others with shaming tactics. After an honest evaluation of how I want the people I love to change, I will apply biblical strategies and patiently await God's work in them.

pray

O God, forgive me for my futile attempts to change others using shame or other corrosive tactics. I have not succeeded in helping others in those ways, but have only added to their problems. From now on, Lord, I want to only use biblical strategies to help others change. Teach me to bless, not curse. Teach me to overcome evil with good. Teach me to instill ownership in others and never enslave them. Father, I now ask Your grace, love, and goodness to be poured out in _____'s life. Let him/her be captured by Your affection, set free by Your mercy, and empowered to be all You've called him/her to be. In Jesus' name, AMEN.

chapter ten

HARDENING of
the OUGHTERIES

When Abby was two, she learned to sing "Jesus loves me this I know, for the Bible tells me so."

She also learned to love French fries.

While dining out on one occasion, Abby detected that I had French fries on my plate while she had none. She began clamoring, "I want French fries! I want French fries!" We declined her request, pointing her to the healthier items on her plate. She continued, "I want French fries!" Still, we did not budge. Finally, in her desperation, she cried out: "I want French fries right now—for the Bible tells me so!"

The Word of God has brought hope to the hurting, light to the lost, and led millions into the saving grace of Jesus Christ. It has also been misused to get everything from French fries to personal relationship control to world political power. Sadly, other than the institution of the family, nothing has caused more shame than institutionalized religion.

I've never been part of a church that handled snakes. I've

never been part of a church that only used Latin. I've never been a part of a church that encouraged ritual sex. And I've never been part of a church that said drinking Coca-Cola is a sin.

But I've been part of almost everything else that calls itself Christian.

I didn't plan it this way, but I grew up in a liturgical church, spent my formative Christian years in conservative fellowships, spent my seminary years and first pastorate in a liberal denomination, and have grown in the Spirit through associations with all kinds of charismatics.

It means that I have been blessed to taste of the richness of almost every stream of the Christian church in America. It also means that I have felt shamed by almost every stream of the Christian church in America.

When I have been in the liturgical church, I have felt like I needed to be more orderly. When I have been among the very conservative, I have felt like I ought to be more holy, and do more witnessing. When I have been among the very liberal, I have felt like I ought to be more accepting of others and that I ought to care more for the poor. Around the charismatics I have always felt like I ought to have more dramatic experiences of the Holy Spirit and, in fact, like I ought to have more of everything.

With all the ways I oughta be better, it's enough to get a case of what one wit calls the "hardening of the oughteries."

I'm always hesitant to say anything negative about the church of Jesus Christ because, in the first place, I'm a pastor and I love the church. For all its flaws and foibles, I love the church. I love the richness of the texture of the body of Christ, and marvel at God's plan that He unfolded among the people called out to be His unique, redeemed possession.

I love the people of God. When my sister-in-law was sick for nine months with the cancer that took her life, my church not only took meals to her every night, they also brought meals to us so we could be free to minister to her. I loved the intimacy of the small church I once pastored, where I went to members' children's birthday parties and sat next to the bed of every person who died. I love the mission of the larger church I pastor now, where we seek to influence a whole city.

Please believe me—I love the church. And I want you to love the church.

So when I say some candid things about the nature of religious shame in the church, I'm not doing so to turn you away from church, but to help you *be* the church as God longs for her to be. I think it's best to find the church that God leads you to and stay there unless the Lord clearly calls you somewhere else.

Having said that, I think it's also fair to say that a church that shames is not really the church at all.

a buffet of religious shame

Sometimes shame-based people are attracted to shame-based churches because it "feels" right to them. But please hear me on this: If shame is your issue, you need to be far, far away from religious condemnation and be in a true church—one that is filled with grace and truth.

Experience one: the formal liturgical church

As a kid growing up in a formal liturgical church, the last thing I would have called church was fun. It felt like the pressure was always on to do church stuff right. Wear the right church clothes. Sit still. Don't make noise.

In our church there was a whole lot of standing up and sitting down. There was also a lot of taking communion, at which time you would kneel. Along with all the requirements of standing, sitting, and kneeling at the right times was an extensive order of service in which you had to follow along and sing the right parts at the right places. At the same time, I couldn't help feeling a little nervous for the minister. He had one of those voices that was just never made for singing—but he had to sing all the time anyway, performing all his parts in all the right slots.

There was one moment each Sunday when I felt really good about church. *When it was over.* I'm not only talking about the simple release from uncomfortable confinement, but also that feeling that I did something kind of good. Something holy. Something out of the ordinary that we were supposed to do. It was sort of like doing something nice for somebody—you might not have really enjoyed doing it, but you felt better about yourself for having done it.

I remember trying to share Christ with a man once who told me that he was Catholic, but that he'd quit going to church some time ago. When I asked him why he had stopped, he replied that he never did like it after they started using English rather than just Latin in the services.

"How interesting," I responded. "Seems to me it would be

more personally meaningful to you if you could actually understand what was being said."

"No," he replied, "it just wasn't special anymore—it just didn't seem holy anymore."

He was a man who had so deeply associated the formality of the order with what it means to be "religious" that it just didn't feel like church if he could actually understand it!

Good liturgical churches help us aspire toward the majesty of Christ and the beauty and order of the Godhead. But as a shame-based person, I couldn't enter into the fullness of a beautiful liturgical service, because I always found my mind focusing more on doing it "right" than actually focusing on the person of Christ.

I learned to value the beauty and power of words early on and, in college, majored in English. I like the eloquence of a formal liturgy. But unhealed of shame, in my early years of ministry I found myself asking "Am I being eloquent?" more than asking "Am I being faithful?"

In any formal church setting, I felt immense pressure to do things right. The first time I preached in the First Presbyterian Church of Atlanta (one of the first times I had ever preached anywhere), I came to the end of what I considered a glorious sermon only to realize that I had no clue what came next in the service. I'd been so focused on delivering my polished sermon that I hadn't given any thought to the transition toward the next part of the service. Panicking, I quickly glanced down at the bulletin and realized there was a hymn coming next so I stammered, "Let's all gather together and sing hymn number...."

My wife has never let me forget that inglorious moment. "What did you want us to do?" she asked laughingly. "*Gather together*? Were we supposed to huddle closer in the pews than we already were?"

She wasn't the only one laughing, though, because she eventually confessed how *she* began my inglorious morning of preaching in the big church. While walking down the storied Peachtree Street from the parking lot to the cement front steps of this venerable Atlanta church, her skirt had slipped down about her knees. Evidently, it hadn't been fastened properly and, completely unaware, she had paraded down the street and into the church with most of her slip showing!

During my days at First Presbyterian, the service began formally with the chiming of the hour. The pastoral staff would be robed and in place a few minutes before 11:00 A.M. At 11:00 A.M. sharp—not 10:59 or 11:01—the organ would sound eleven chimes. We would count the chimes and, on the seventh chime, stand. Our standing was the cue for the congregation to stand also.

After the eleventh chime, the organist proceeded immediately with the doxology. On one occasion when the senior pastor was out of town, the associates and I were a bit slow getting into the sanctuary. We knew that the organist would chime the hour at 11:00 A.M. whether we were in our places or not. We also knew that from the organ loft the organist couldn't see whether we were in our places! What would happen after the chiming? Would everyone stand anyway? Would they start singing the doxology without us? Imagine a motley assortment of associate pastors scooting into place while the congregation was half finished singing the doxology!

It took me years of healing to become less concerned with doing things in church "right" and more concerned with doing the right thing in church. In other words, sometimes the right thing is to "mess up"—to just not know what to do. Sometimes the right thing is to weep or groan with sighs too deep for words. Sometimes the right thing is to be silent. Sometimes the right thing is to violate every tradition and norm in order to show value to an individual or honor to the awesome presence of God.

In a particularly shameful moment, one of my seminary professors made fun of people who pray "I just want to thank You, Jesus." It wasn't just an attack against pietistic Christians, it was a mockery of anything less than eloquent prayers. Granted, "I just want to thank You, Jesus" doesn't compare to the grandeur of the Book of Common Prayer or to Augustus Toplady's majestic hymns of grace. But God cares more about the heart than anything else. If you have ever felt that church was all about sounding good and doing things right, shame off you! People look upon the outward appearance, but the Lord looks upon the heart (1 Samuel 16:7).

Experience two: the conservative Bible church

After my experience in the liturgical church of my upbringing, my broken family began attending an evangelical church with one of the greatest Bible preachers I've ever known. I loved that church. Even as a teenager, if I had to drive myself to church, I would go, sit in the back, and listen to Roy Putnam preach the Word of God.

During that same time in my life, I also became heavily involved in an evangelical parachurch ministry. It was there that I developed true Christian friends and learned that Christianity is about a relationship with God through Jesus Christ. In college, I was again involved in an evangelical campus ministry and attended a conservative Bible church.

It was in those fellowships that I learned the importance of having a "quiet time"—a daily time with God through reading Scripture and praying. My Christian friends and I held one another accountable with our recurrent question, "Are you having good quiet times?" It felt really good to tell a Bible study leader, "I've had a quiet time every day this week!" Oppositely, I felt really bad if I had to report, "I've not had regular quiet times lately." Once I remember gasping as if I'd heard the confession of a serial rapist when a respected Christian student dared to declare: "I haven't had a good quiet time in months."

We talked a lot about how much better our day went if we had that quiet time in the morning. Well, that in itself made me feel guilty because I'm no morning person. I think that it *is* good to get up and, first thing, spend time alone with God. There *is* something precious about the early morning dew of God's presence.

But honestly, *my* best moments with God had come late at night.

Somewhere along the way, however, I figured myself to be less spiritual because I didn't have a crane to get me out of bed at 5:30 A.M. so I could spend time with God. What's worse, I began feeling sort of doomed if I didn't have my quiet time. I sort of expected the day to go poorly if I hadn't read the Bible and prayed that morning.

My experience in the evangelical fellowships helped me value God's Word, but my shame kept me from entering into the true depth of what life with God can be. I was more devoted to studying God's Word than *experiencing* God's Word. Page after page after page in the Bible tells us how to live. We're supposed to give a lot, have a lot of joy, and do right things in the world. But simply *knowing* that we ought to be generous, joyful, and just is a far cry from *being* generous, joyful, and just.

Most Bible churches and conservative Bible fellowships place great emphasis on the study of Scripture but say little about the power of God to transform, heal, and fill our lives with joy. It wasn't until I learned about the role of the Holy Spirit from my charismatic friends that I experienced the open floodgate of love, joy, and power that can fill a Christian's life. Now, as a preacher of the gospel, I find it cruel to tell a person how they ought to live and not give them the opportunity to be filled with the empowering presence of God that will *enable* them to live as the Bible says we should.

I have known many Christians who grew up in the kind of conservative churches that place a high priority on individual holiness and morality. My mother's father was a Methodist minister who believed it wrong to drink Coca-Cola. I have an uncle whose church split over whether the church should sing only Psalms or should dare to sing "human" hymns also. I cried when I once ministered to a woman who had been molested as a child and whose church, upon learning about her molestation, disallowed her from serving in children's ministry because she had been "tainted."

Churches that emphasize morality and behavior can become rather arbitrary in what they emphasize. I once drove by a church named "One Way Bible Church." My friend laughed and remarked, "Yeah, one way. *Our* way!" A friend recently applied to teach at a conservative church school in our city. It's a good church and a respected school and I know she'd make a great teacher.

But they refused to accept her.

There was a line in the contract that said that she would pledge never to drink an alcoholic beverage. She couldn't honestly say that she would never have a glass of wine with a nice meal. As one who has been hurt first hand by alcohol abuse, it'd be all right with me if everybody decided to teetotal. My point isn't to argue whether drinking wine is forbidden in Scripture (though it is nearly impossible to say so). Rather, what puzzles me is how arbitrary that particular potential vice is. I mean, why a clause in the contract about not drinking alcohol? What about all the other, clearer, laws of Scripture?

Is there a clause that says I won't ever gossip?

Is there a clause that says I won't overeat?

Is there a clause that says I will never violate the speed limit, since the Bible says to obey the laws of the land?

Why do we pick out certain behaviors for our scrutiny?

Philip Yancey tells about a woman who spent a segment of her life in prostitution. Sometime after she had quit that way of life she was asked, "While you were hurting, looking for answers, and still prostituting, did you ever think about going to church?" Her answer is an indictment: "Church? Why would I go to church? They would have just made me feel worse about myself."

Moralistic, behavior-oriented churches can shame us with the basic message, "You aren't acceptable until your behavior matches the Bible in every way." Traditionally, the church has conveyed this order of events:

- Behave properly;
- Believe all the right things;
- Belong to the fellowship.

But Jesus seems to have reversed the order. He was called the "Friend of sinners" because He associated so often with people who didn't behave or believe rightly. In fact, you could be Jesus' close friend before you had shown any change in your behavior or belief system. The fishermen and tax collectors He called into discipleship were not morally upright people—and certainly weren't the scriptural scholars of the day.

But Jesus wanted a relationship with them.

Out of their friendship with Him, they began to see life differently. Through their daily encounters with the Word in flesh, they were learning the Word. Their behaviors changed some while Jesus was with them, but even after Jesus had died for them, they were frightened doubters until the Holy Spirit filled their spirits with boldness and fire.

With Jesus, the order was: *Belong, Believe, Behave.* Certainly, Jesus never condoned sin nor promoted unbelief. He was insistent that the Truth was narrowly focused in His own

Personhood and insisted that His followers "sin no more." But He wants to be your Friend not because you believe the right things or do the right things—He just wants to be your Friend because He loves you. He wants to be your Friend, period.

Conservative churches can become so concerned with biblical truth and morality that they, like the Pharisees, miss the whole point of the Scriptures. The Pharisees, intent on not accidentally ingesting a small bug, which would be a ceremonially unclean creature, strained their wine. But Jesus rebuked them for swallowing camels by missing out on the priority of God's Word—love for God and love for one another.

I love God's Word because God's breath is in it. Like the psalmist, I love to meditate upon His law day and night. But I don't worship the Bible, I worship God. Christianity is not primarily about believing all the right things nor is it about doing all the right things. It is primarily about belonging to God. If you have felt doomed by your chronic behavioral problems or your inadequate knowledge of the Bible, shame off you! Christianity is not about a striving to measure up to someone's holy standard. It's about surrendering to the One who already loves you—just the way you are.

Experience three: the liberal mainline church

After my valuable years in conservative churches and Bible fellowships, I was somehow led into a mainline denomination. The Presbyterian Church (USA) is, by any standard, a leader in liberal causes. While (like every denomination) the PCUSA has a diversity of theological views in both pew and pulpit, its hierarchy and seminaries are theologically liberal. By theologically liberal I simply mean that they value progressive thought about the interpretation of Scriptures, and place more emphasis on societal justice than on personal piety.

The beauty of liberalism is its value of acceptance. Unwelcome in many conservative churches, homosexuals, intellectual skeptics, and people with a past of moral failure gravitate to churches where there is more emphasis on loving acceptance than there is on the moral message of the Bible.

Feeling called to the Presbyterian Church (USA) at that time in my life, I decided it was best to attend one of the denominational seminaries. While there, I developed some very close friendships with both professors and students, learned a lot—and also pondered escaping to attend a more conservative seminary almost every day!

Whereas in conservative churches I felt like I didn't behave or believe rightly enough, in the liberal church, I felt condemned for believing anything or asserting that any behavior was better than another. I once took a doctorate level course in marriage therapy. One of our assignments was to write an essay using a biblical image for marriage. I chose the image of covenant. My simple essay explained that covenant is a permanent commitment seated in choice.

The point was clear: Even though sometimes marriage gets difficult, I stay married because I have made a covenant with God and my wife, until death do us part.

When I finished sharing my essay with the class, a female student, who had experienced three divorces, scoffed at me, saying: "Your problem is that you're just not willing to accept a failed marriage." What?!—now I have to feel ashamed that my marriage *hasn't* failed? In a conservative church, you might get rejected for being divorced, but now I found myself in a liberal setting that seemed to value divorce because the divorcees were more open to admit their failures!

Also, as strange as it sounds, I sometimes felt guilty for having it too easy in life. After all, I am a white male American. I have every advantage in the world. I haven't been persecuted for my race or oppressed for my gender. I'm the one who has always had the position of ease, power, and control in society. My experience in the liberal church left me feeling like I was just too rich, too white, too American, and too male. Sometimes I wanted to cry out and say, "I can't help it—I *am* a white American male—as despicable as that is—I'm stuck with it. Can't you like me anyway?"

I already felt ashamed of being too prosperous. I wasn't rich by most American's standards. But by the standards of the whole world, how could a young man with two cars and a decent house not be called rich? I already assumed that Jesus' camel and eye-of-the-needle story applied to me—and it was going to be hard for me to get into heaven anyway.

But the liberals in my seminary, in their noble consciousness for social justice, made me feel worse. True, their advocacy for the poor prompted some deeper compassion in me. But mainly I just felt bad about myself that I hadn't given all my money to the poor. My wife was volunteering at the women's shelter. I had refused to take the most prestigious and generous scholarship that the seminary offered. I said no when a benefactor at First Presbyterian Church wanted to pay for my education. But despite my best efforts, I felt like I wasn't doing enough for the poor.

If you have ever felt that you just weren't caring enough or that you were too prosperous or that you were too concerned about personal piety, shame off you! Christianity is no more about doing the list of liberal things than it is the list of conservative things. Learn, stretch, grow—but forget thinking that you can ever give away enough or do enough to solve all the world's ills.

Experience four: the charismatic fellowship

Finally, there is my experience with charismatic Christianity. I don't particularly like using the word *charismatic*. In the first place, every Christian has the "charismata," the gifts of the Holy Spirit, and is, therefore, charismatic. Thankfully the word is fading from our language because of all the various baggage attached to it. But for the sake of discussion, when I say charismatic, I mean that segment of the body of Christ that values the present-day work of the Holy Spirit as expressed in supernatural manifestations and gifts.

When I was in college, my evangelical Bible study group had set out to explore the role of the Holy Spirit, and we decided to attend a charismatic meeting on campus together. A healing evangelist was being hosted by a charismatic fellowship. The meeting had lively worship and healing prayer for the sick. Then, toward the end, the evangelist asked if there was anybody who hadn't received the baptism of the Holy Spirit who would like to do so. With every head bowed and every eye closed (except mine), I observed that all eight people in my Bible study group raised their hands. We were the *only* ones who raised our hands.

The evangelist said, "There—a whole row. Come forward." And so we did.

Once up front, several excited students gathered around me and began laying hands on me. I had the distinct feeling that they were quite tickled to have some "fresh meat." One person was praying in tongues (which I had never heard before) while another was laying his hands on my stomach and reciting "Out of your belly shall flow rivers of living water." I thought, *Brother, if you don't stop pushing on my stomach like that, something is going to flow forth from my belly—and it's not going to be living water!*

They kept praying, pushing, and pleading with me to pray in tongues. You can be sure, the last thing I was going to do at that moment was pray in tongues. It's hard to have a profound spiritual experience when all you're meditating on is the nearest exit!

Before we had gone to the meeting, a friend had told some members of our group, "Remember, you're just as good of Christians as they are." I had thought, *Why do you need to tell us that?*

After going, I understood.

It wasn't that anyone in the meeting was openly unkind or arrogant. Quite the opposite—they were full of joy, enthusiasm, and received us eagerly. But after people pray and push on your stomach for a while, you can't help feeling like you've disappointed them a bit if no living water flows out of your belly.

To my amazement, one person from our Bible study was quite touched by the Holy Spirit that evening. Her name was Anne and she later became my wife.

"In that zoo?!" I asked her. "How could you be touched by the Lord in the midst of all the pushing and prodding?" There I was, shaming her for getting the very experience that I wanted but didn't get. Anne was always kind of quiet about exactly what happened to her that evening, but I knew that she was changed. It began a great longing within me to have the fullness of whatever blessing and empowerment there is to have from God.

Hungering for deeper experiences of God is a good thing. In fact, we are commended in Scripture for hungering and thirsting for God and His righteousness. But how do you feel when you've asked God for a blessing that you've yet to receive, though you've seen others receive it? You can start feeling like a "have not."

I'm convinced that every major move of God has eventually waned because participants overemphasized the importance of a manifestation of the Holy Spirit. Emphasis on manifestations sets up an environment of shame that eventually turns masses of people away and grieves the Holy Spirit. In my lifetime, we've had a variety of genuine outpourings of the Spirit that have blessed thousands and left thousands feeling like they don't measure up. We have had moves of God in which the gift of tongues became the spiritual barometer. We have had moves in which "claiming a healing" became the test of true spirituality. In others, it's been about being "slain in the Spirit." Supernatural joy and laughter has served as another line of division.

I once heard an international missionary share about his experience among a group of Christians that began to experience God's presence so powerfully that some of them began to actually glow. Literally, there was some sort of radiance upon their countenance not unlike Moses' face after Mount Sinai. An extraordinary move of God occurred among that ethnicity and many people came to faith through it.

Several years later, however, the missionary traveled back to that part of the world and, to his sadness, discovered that a deep fracture had occurred in the body of Christ there.

You guessed it—"the glows" versus the "no glows."

Though I felt ashamed that I didn't "get it" at that first charismatic meeting, I did continue to thirst for more of God. Some time later that year, in the quietness of my own prayer closet, I had an encounter with God's Spirit that truly intoxicated me with joy, brought clarity to my faith, and empowered me with gifts I didn't have before.

When you experience something wonderful, you naturally want others to experience it, too. I think that's why those charismatic Christians pushed on my stomach and pleaded with me to pray in tongues. I think it's why someone who has been supernaturally healed has special faith to believe for someone else's healing. There's nothing wrong with wanting something good to happen to someone else. But at some point, the proclamation of what is available turns to shame for those who don't have it.

No one has ever told me that I was less important, less valuable, or less of a Christian if I didn't have a certain gift or manifestation, but that's what my filter of shame surmised from my early experience in charismatic meetings.

I could sum up my shame sentiments among charismatics in a simple phrase, *I ought to have more*. I ought to have more joy. I ought to have more healing. I ought to have more prosperity. I ought to have more gifts. I ought to have more manifestations. I ought to have more supernatural experiences.

If you've ever felt like a "have not" in the midst of other Christians—shame off you! No two people will have all the same experiences of God. There's no need to ever compare your experience of God with someone else's. Please be free from trying to perform spiritually in order to be accepted. You're already accepted by God, and you don't need any sort of spiritual badge to prove it. As you let go of the pressure to be like other Christians, just humbling yourself before God, you'll find that He will fill you with good gifts.

approachable as jesus

Why did people flock to Jesus? I have come to one, simple conclusion: He wasn't at all like the other religious leaders of His day. He was a Rabbi, a "religious" Leader and Healer, but He didn't make people feel worse about themselves. There was something so approachable about Jesus that even the worst "sinners" felt safe to approach Him. He said some very narrow things—pointing to one way, one truth, and one life in Himself. Yet no one ever felt shamed or condemned by His demeanor. (Unless it was the tyrannical, super-legalists who oppressed the people in the name of God.)

People have always longed for eternal truth, mystery, and power, but they have been willing to forfeit their spiritual search for the sake of avoiding shame. For the first time, in Jesus Christ, truth, mystery, and power became available without shame. When the truth is presented in perfect grace, myriads will flock to behold it.

Jesus Christ was full of grace and full of truth. He wasn't 50 percent truth and 50 percent grace. He wasn't sometimes gracious and sometimes truthful. At every moment and in every encounter, Jesus Christ was fully loving and fully real. There are some people, of course, who don't want to hear the truth that will call them to repent. But most people want truth—as long as they can hear it without shame. No one wants to feel condemned.

As soon as a soul feels condemnation, the heart closes up to protect itself. If the message of the gospel is in any way clouded by a message of shame, then people will avoid church at all costs. If, however, there is a church that proclaims eternal truth and mystery in the context of utter love and acceptance, that church will find the world at its door.

God has entrusted His mystery, truth, and power to the church of Jesus Christ saying, "Freely you have received. Freely give." When we directly or indirectly communicate "You must behave differently or believe differently before we will share the mystery, truth, and power of Christ with you," we have made the gospel something less than free, and we have used our knowledge or spiritual power to shame others.

As a pastor, I know how tempting it is to lay guilt on parishioners. We want people to be better Christians. We want them to be more generous, to read their Bible more, to pray more, give more, and to live more ethically. We know that we can spur them to act more Christian-like by telling them that they don't measure up and that God's not pleased with them. Desperate to be loved by God and to be accepted by the church, some people will change their behaviors. But masses of people will avoid us at all costs.

WHEN YOU NEED GOOD NEWS

Culture's perception of the church is betrayed by its understanding of the word *preach*. If a teenager is disgusted with his parents' exhortations he might say, "I wish you'd quit preaching at me all the time." If someone says, "quit preaching," it means "Quit telling me what to do—quit acting so self-righteous, and quit trying to make me feel bad about myself."

I lament the loss of the word *preach*. To preach is to proclaim the gospel of Jesus Christ. The gospel is, literally, the "good news." If I'm discouraged, that's when I most need a preacher! If I'm struggling with a sense of guilt and condemnation, that's when I most *need* a messenger of good news!

Who doesn't need the good news? It's good news for the poor. Good news for the brokenhearted. Good news for the alcoholic. Good news for the fearful. Good news for the depressed. Good news for those who've failed. Good news for the skeptic. Good news for the lonely. Good news for "sinners." How sad and ironic: the gospel's message can be summarized: "Because of Christ, your sins and failures don't define you. Shame off you!" Yet it is so often perceived (and proclaimed) as the exact opposite: "Because of your sins and failures, shame on you."

The path to real revival is for the glorious church of Jesus Christ to become more as He is. Oh church, let us be as Jesus is—full of grace and truth. Most people are not avoiding our gospel, they are avoiding *us*. Let's proclaim Jesus as He truly is. Clear truth. Love with no strings attached. A Friend to anyone, regardless of their beliefs and behaviors.

Let's lift Jesus up for who He is and watch the Father draw people unto Him. Show Him to be the One who bears our shame, not bestows it, and watch people draw near to Him. Let's tell a thirsting world, shame off you!

ASK   A Question to Inquire:

How have I felt shamed in religious organizations? How have I used religious shame against others?

BELIEVE   A Principle to Ponder:

"The path to real revival is for the glorious church of Jesus Christ to become more as He is. Oh church, let us be as Jesus is—full of grace and truth. Most people are not avoiding our gospel, they are avoiding *us*. Let's proclaim Jesus as He truly is."

The temptation for Christian organizations is to utilize shame in order to get people to be more Christlike. But Christ Himself did not use shame. Instead, the truth He shared was flooded with an immensely attractive stream of grace.

CHOOSE A Commitment to Keep:

I choose today to forgive churches, pastors, friends, and religious organizations that have contributed to my shame. I choose today to invite the Spirit of Jesus Christ to minister to others in a shame-free way. I choose to help my church be more like Christ—full of grace and truth.

PRAY

*O God, grant me the grace to forgive those
who have used religion to shame me, and grant me
the grace to face how I have done the same. I thank You
that Jesus Christ came full of grace and truth. Make me
full of His grace and full of His truth. Make me more
like Christ that I might be used in bringing the hope
of the gospel to others. In Jesus' name, AMEN.*

CHAPTER ELEVEN

THE HIGHEST VISTA OF ALL

The Blue Ridge Mountains of North Carolina put on an annual display of God's artistry. Fall telegraphs its yearly summons to the oaks and elms and maples, *"Let the fireworks begin!"*

And so they do, in silent, stunning explosions of gold, orange, and fiery red.

One year Anne and I rented a sporty convertible just to make the ascension on the Blue Ridge Parkway. As you begin the climb and negotiate the gentle curves along this storied highway, the view on one side is obstructed by a granite wall, and on the other side by the density of trees.

Until...

Suddenly...

You round a bend and, behold, a wide vista opens up before you—the valley and the ridge beyond. Pulling off to the side of the road you pause there, gathering your breath, to watch the sunlight dance upon the crimson and lemony hues.

Thinking you have found "the spot," the very best place for viewing the glorious display, you drive on with reluctance. (How could it get any better?) That's the way we felt that sunny autumn day, soaking in the view from our open-roofed rental. Driving on, you keep climbing and climbing. Again, momentarily, the view is hindered, but you round yet another turn and—another vista, higher and even more brilliant than the first. Just when you thought the colors could not be more magnificently painted on the landscape of the valley below, you realize that you have come to an even more wondrous point of perspective.

After a long pause at the paved turnout, you leave that scenic overlook with strange anticipation. Perhaps there is an even more sublime pinnacle from which the whole glory of the ridge can be surveyed in all its richness. Perhaps you will be able to gaze into the blueness of far horizons.

And that's just what happens.

As you ascend, the breathtaking beauty keeps increasing in splendor. At the top of that climb, you pull over to park next to a grassy overlook. You spread your blanket and pull out your sandwich or fried chicken for your picnic, but you know that the real nourishment is the panorama all about you. And even while you feed upon that beauty, you know that it extends farther than your eyes can see. To view any more of its splendor, you would need a new set of eyes that could see further, that could differentiate layers of the color spectrum with greater subtlety, and could let in more of the brilliant light of the sun on such a crisp day.

But why go on? You've climbed to the true vista of the parkway, and you dare not move until you've seen all you can see.

The theological truth I'm about to share is that Blue Ridge vista to me. I had glimpsed the beauty—the sheer radiance— of God's grace many times before. I knew I hadn't seen it all, and could never see it all in this life. But I had no idea what awaited me when I made one more ascending turn on the park- way of my understanding. The vista that opened up to me—the astonishing beauty of the New Covenant sprawling out before the eyes of my heart—made me cry out in wonder.

It was too good to be true. Yet it is true.

I stopped there, at that wide overlook, and began to feast. And I've been feasting ever since. Somewhere, there may be a higher vista still, but I cannot imagine it, and I have not left this glorious viewpoint. It's too breathtaking. Too life-changing.

And if you will come…I want to take you there.

Be my traveling companion for these next few pages. We will ascend, negotiate a few sharp curves (please stay with me), and then I will show you the scene that has changed my under- standing of the gospel forever. If you come with me, and if you see this sublime sight, it will do more to heal your shame than a thousand books, seminars, or counseling sessions. Come, see why the New Covenant is so new…and how it can make you new as well.

a bargain with the gods

A little boy foolishly playing on a rooftop began sliding down its steep pitch toward some major bruises, or worse, below. As he was slipping down the shingles, he cried out:

"Lord, save me! If You save me, I'll become a missionary!"

About the time he finished hollering out his vow, his jeans snagged on a nail head protruding from a shingle, immediately halting his descent. Relieved, the boy looked heavenward again and retracted, "Never mind, Lord, this nail saved me."

Almost every civilization, at every time, has had some notion of covenant. A solemn agreement that, at its heart, asserts, "If you will do A, then I will do B." The most common form of covenant on historical record is a political/military covenant in which a larger, more powerful nation would make an agreement with a lesser nation. Small, weak entities knew they were vulnerable and needed defense. Large empires didn't want the smaller governments surrounding their own nation to align themselves with the empire's enemies. Characteristically, the powerful nation would promise protection to the small country and, in return, the weaker nation would promise not to join forces with the opposition.

In a similar fashion, anthropologists have learned that almost all peoples at all times have made various sorts of covenants with their gods. Why? Because all human beings have a deep sense that there is something more powerful than they.[13] When you are in a position of weakness, you instinctively want to strike some sort of bargain with that stronger power. For a boy falling off a roof, it might be the promise of missionary service. For the worshippers of Baal, it might mean cutting their own flesh.[14]

The vast majority of all religious notions have been rooted in this desperate longing to strike a bargain with the higher power of the universe. And when you boil it down, most

Christians have adopted a religious system that essentially asserts that same theme: *God, I pledge to align myself with You, if You will, in return, pledge to protect and bless me.*

The question in ancient times was not, *Should I align myself with a higher power?* The question was *Who is the highest power?* The essential drama of the whole Old Testament narrative hangs upon that question. *We are weak and powerless. We must find protection and blessing from someone. Who has the most power? With whom shall we align ourselves? Is it Pharaoh or Moses? The sun god or Yahweh? If Moses is on the mountaintop too long, maybe we can cut a deal with a golden calf to supplement the covenant we already have.*

climbing toward the vista

This one true God revealed Himself to Moses, first through a burning bush, and then through a burning mountaintop intimacy. At Mount Sinai,

> Moses went up to God, and the LORD called to him from the mountain and said, "This is what you are to say to the house of Jacob and what you are to tell the people of Israel: 'You yourselves have seen what I did to Egypt, and how I carried you on eagles' wings and brought you to myself. Now if you obey me fully and keep my covenant, then out of all nations you will be my treasured possession. Although the whole earth is mine, you will be for me a kingdom of priests and a holy nation.'" (Exodus 19:3–6)

The covenant of the law (the Old Covenant) couldn't be simpler. God said, "You have seen that I am the Lord and no one has power over Me. I do not want you to align yourselves with pagan gods. If you will align yourself fully with Me, then I will protect and bless you always."

The people received Jehovah's covenant offer with gratitude: "When Moses went and told the people all the LORD'S words and laws, they responded with one voice, 'All that the LORD has spoken we will do'" (19:8). The covenant was confirmed as Moses set up an altar and had young Israelite men offer animal sacrifices to the Lord.

The covenant was sealed with a shared meal: "Moses and Aaron, Nadab and Abihu, and the seventy elders of Israel went up and...saw God...and they ate and drank" (Exodus 24:9–11).

Please stay with me here. We're on that Blue Ridge Parkway heading for a stunning vista. But we have a few more turns to go.

Almost all covenants hold five elements in common: 1) representatives for each side; 2) binding oaths; 3) promises of blessings/benefits; 4) blood sacrifice; 5) a shared meal. The covenant of the law demonstrates these elements clearly. 1) The representatives were Jehovah and Moses; 2) the oaths were God's pledge to keep Israel as His people and Israel's pledge to keep God's law; 3) the benefit to God was His own glory while the benefit to Israel was their prosperity and security; 4) the blood sacrifices were bulls upon an altar of twelve stones; 5) the shared meal included seventy elders in the presence of God.

The Old Covenant was a marvelous gift to a weak and fledgling people. Those who had been no people were made God's people! Those who had no land of their own would be given a land flowing with milk and honey. Slaves would become owners. The rejected and oppressed would become the favored. What a glorious gift!

And with the unspeakable benefits of being a covenant partner with Jehovah, the Hebrews received yet another gift—the law. The law itself was a remarkable blessing because an all-knowing God gave clear instructions to His people about morality, societal order, and even instructions for personal health and welfare. Can you imagine how valuable it was to be the only people in the world who knew it was a good idea to wash your hands before you eat? Or that you should quarantine a person with an infectious disease?

Of course, the Israelites, like all the other ancient civilizations, had no concept of bacteria or how infections spread, but they had the revelation of the law. The psalmist can rightly say: "I will walk about in freedom, for I have sought out your precepts...for I delight in your commands because I love them" (Psalm 119:45, 47).

If belonging to God and walking in the light of God's revelation was a blessing, what's even more remarkable is that God gave the Hebrews a way to make amends when they didn't hold up their end of the covenant. God established a system of sacrifices by which the priests could slaughter innocent animals on behalf of the sinful people. God's wrath against covenant breakers would be temporarily shifted away from the human sinners and onto the innocent animal. Every time they broke the covenant, the Hebrews deserved to lose their divine covering and their special standing as God's people. But God, in His mercy, allowed the debt of the covenant breakers to be partially paid through the sacrifice of animals.

If you have entered a mortgage agreement with a bank for your house and you get behind on the payments, you will be thankful if the bank will allow you to make a partial payment without foreclosing on you. If you don't make your full payments, the bank has a right to remove you from your home. Any other temporary arrangement by which you get to keep the house demonstrates mercy on the lender's part. The sacrificial system in the Old Covenant was a merciful provision from a merciful God.

In summary, almost all people throughout history have sought an agreement with a higher power for protection and blessing. The Old Testament records the story of the covenant God made with Israel by which Israel would be the treasured possession of the one true God. That same narrative also tells of the recurring failure of God's people to keep their side of the covenant. Their continued violation of God's law and their recurring idolatry led to their eventual exile, but God could not forget His people. For century upon century, sacrifice after sacrifice, God's wrath was poured out on innocent animals instead of the guilty people, and He promised His beloved a better way that was to come.

a new and better way

The new way was most famously forecast by the prophet Jeremiah:

"The time is coming," declares the LORD,
"when I will make a new covenant
with the house of Israel
and with the house of Judah.
It will not be like the covenant
I made with their forefathers...
This is the covenant I will make...
I will put my law in their minds
and write it on their hearts." (Jeremiah
31:31–33)

A New Covenant. A different covenant. A better covenant. What a day that would be! In fact, it's the very day that you and I are living right now.

When I became a Christian as a young person, relief and joy surged through my heart. Early on I came to understand that we are no longer under the covenant of the law. I knew that good works can't save us, but only grace through faith. I was taught that Christianity isn't about a set of rules, but about a relationship with Jesus Christ.

Thankfully, I was taught early in my Christian life how to have a daily quiet time, reading Scripture, and praying. I was also thankful to learn that God has a plan for my life that, if followed, would make life go much better for me. Through my sense of personal relationship with Christ, I had an assurance that as a Christian I belonged to God and was special to Him. I had confidence that I would one day go to heaven and be with Him. I found that if I kept a daily quiet time, I had more peace and felt more confident and settled in my day. Life went better for me when I filled my mind with God's Word.

And I surely found out that it's better to follow God's plan for morality than the world's! I decided not to sneak out with classmates and secretly get drunk at parties. My Christian friends and I had a much better time than those who were coming home in the middle of the night, throwing up, and getting punished. Likewise, I decided not to have sexual intercourse until I was married. It's so worth it! I never had to worry about a girl telling me she was pregnant. Never had to worry about discovering a lifelong disease.

I also decided early on that I would try to be nice to people. I found out if I would treat others with kindness, they would be more likely to treat me kindly. Life as a Christian for me was so much better than what I saw in non-Christian's lives. I had a sense of belonging to God. I had direction for my life through regular prayer and Scripture reading. I had the blessings that come from living a basically moral life. Everything about being a Christian was great. Lifelong belonging. Life-grounding belief. Life-rewarding behavior. It was all wonderful. Nothing about it was bad.

But what about it was so *new*?

After all, Israel, under the Old Covenant, had a sense of belonging to God. They, under the law, discovered that if they delighted in the Word of God, then life would go better for them. And the Old Covenant people certainly knew the benefit of living according to God's standards of morality.

As good as my idea of Christian covenant was, what made this covenant *new* and *better* than the old? Sure, I didn't have to go to the trouble of offering bulls on stone altars. It was nice

not to have to bring a turtledove with me to church. I was glad
not to have to go to a priest and get some blood sprinkled on
me. But I have to admit, I viewed my daily quiet time as a sacrifice. I was giving up time that I could have spent on myself.
And admittedly, there were seasons in my life in which I felt a
bit jinxed if I didn't keep my quiet time. If I had a bad day, I
would often look back and realize, "Well, I just didn't spend
any time with God today, that was the problem." And though
I didn't fear getting exiled to Babylon, I knew times of haunting
guilt over the things that I did wrong. I didn't have extra-marital
intercourse with a woman, but how many times had I lusted?
Didn't Jesus call that adultery, too?

Wasn't my "new" covenant just a modified old covenant?
Wasn't my personal experience of Jesus Christ just my way of
knowing I belonged to God—but not altogether different from
Moses' burning bush encounter that gave him a relationship
with God? Wasn't my commitment to daily "quiet time" just a
New Testament version of an Old Testament truth, "Blessed
are they who keep his statutes and seek him with all their
heart"? (Psalm 119:2). Wasn't my Christian morality just an
updated model of the Hebraic ethic, "Blessed is the man who
does not walk in the counsel of the wicked or stand in the way
of sinners or sit in the seat of mockers"? (Psalm 1:1).

If you are a Christian, you are under a New Covenant, one
that the writer of Hebrews calls altogether better than the old.
But what about the Christian life is so categorically new?

Don't misunderstand—I was thankful for my version of the
Christian life and it would be worth having, because it insured
me a better life on earth and eternity with God. But it wasn't

enough! I mean, it didn't match up with what I saw in someone like Paul, who knew himself to be more than a conqueror. Mainly I had to ask: If my Christian faith was so new, so much better than that of the Old Covenant, *why did I still have so much shame?*

WHY NEW IS NEW

Come with me. Feel the fall breeze upon your face. We're on the Blue Ridge, making the curve. We're approaching the vista. Get ready to behold it. It's why the New Covenant is so incomprehensibly new. It's why the Good News is so unbelievably good. Breathe deep—it's breathtaking.

The New Covenant has all the characteristics of a biblical covenant (two representatives; binding oaths; benefits; blood sacrifice; shared meal).

But there has never, never been a covenant like this new one.

The two representatives are still divine and human. But please hear this: *The New Covenant is not between you and God.* You are not the primary representative on the earthly side.

Jesus is.

And who represents the divine side of this covenant?

Jesus, again.

Scripture declares, "For there is one God and one Mediator between God and men, the Man Christ Jesus" (1 Timothy 2:5, NKJV). "But now He has obtained a more excellent ministry, inasmuch as He is also Mediator of a better covenant, which was established on better promises" (Hebrews 8:6, NKJV).

The New Covenant is new because it's not between you and God.

It's between God the Son and God the Father.

In one person, Jesus Christ, humanity and divinity meet. "The Word was with God and the Word was God...and the Word became flesh" (John 1:1, 14, NKJV). Jesus is THE Man who represents you in the New Covenant, and Jesus is THE fullness of God Himself who represents the triune God.

Yes, there are two representatives in the New Covenant, one divine, one human. But you are totally out of the drama. You're out of the loop. There is one and only one Mediator between God and humanity. And you are not He. The New Covenant is totally new because it is not between God and His people, but between God and His Son.

The New Covenant also has solemn oaths.

But they are not your oaths.

The Son pledges to live in perfect obedience to the Father's will. The Father pledges to bless and highly exalt the Son over all things. The Son pledges to always say no to Satan and to always say yes to the Father. The Father pledges not to withhold any measure of the Holy Spirit from the Son, and to give Him all authority in heaven and on earth.

The Son never breaks His oath. The Son, even when He bleeds sweat in Gethsemane, is committed to the oath: "My Father, if it is not possible for this cup to be taken away unless I drink it, may your will be done" (Matthew 26:42). Even unto death itself and even unto the most shameful form of death, the Son keeps His oath: "And being found in appearance as a man, he humbled himself and became obedient to death—even death on a cross" (Philippians 2:8).

The Father never breaks His oath to His Son. "Therefore God exalted him to the highest place and gave him the name that is above every name, that at the name of Jesus every knee should bow...and every tongue confess that Jesus Christ is Lord..." (vv. 9–11).

When the Covenant-keeping Christ calls out on the cross, "It is finished," He is announcing to all the cosmos that the covenant has been completed!

Sealed. Delivered. Forever.

The New Covenant is not like the old, subject to violation and suspension, because the New Covenant has been made and kept in the one Man, Jesus Christ. He is the God who issues unlimited blessing, and He is the human person who fulfills all righteousness.

Are you seeing the stunning beauty of this vista? Are you taking in its magnificence? The New Covenant does not hinge upon your faithfulness. It all hangs upon the faithfulness of Jesus Christ. "God is faithful, by whom you were called into the fellowship of His Son, Jesus Christ our Lord" (1 Corinthians 1:9, NKJV). "But the Lord is faithful, who will establish you and guard you from the evil one" (2 Thessalonians 3:3, NKJV).

There is no drama between a faithful God and an unfaithful people. The drama was between the Father and the Son. Would the Son remain obedient, even unto a shameful, agonizing cross? Would the Father have the power to fulfill his oath to raise the Son from the dead and highly exalt Him? There is no wondering whether the New Covenant will be kept—it *has* been kept. There is no possibility that the New

Covenant will fail because it has been made and kept in the one Man Jesus Christ, and He has risen to take His rightful throne.

Nothing, nothing, nothing can undo the perfect fulfillment of the New Covenant by Jesus Christ nor the perfect exaltation of the Covenant Keeper.

So how do you and I benefit from this covenant?

the mystery revealed

Here is the mystery of God's plan revealed. Here is the vista that pales every other vista in all the world, in all of time. Just as Jeremiah prophesied, the New Covenant is not like the Old. Something happens inside of you when you become a Christian.

Call it being born anew.

Call it being transformed by the renewing of your mind.

Call it Jesus taking up residence in your heart.

Whatever you call it, an unthinkable exchange takes place. Suddenly, you are joined into Christ Himself. He is the firstborn of many, and you and I are His brothers and sisters. We suddenly change position in life. We become coheirs with Christ. "God made him who had no sin to be sin for us, so that in him we might become the righteousness of God" (2 Corinthians 5:21). Suddenly, your old, guilt-ridden life died away and your new life was completely embedded into Christ. "For you died, and your life is now hidden with Christ in God" (Colossians 3:3).

It means that the Christian life is in no way a modified version of the Old Covenant. It is not an improved, slightly revised, newly updated covenant. It is categorically new. It means that our role is not to keep the covenant, but to abide in the One who has already kept the covenant (John 15).

Do you see the difference? You and I are *not* called to spend our lives trying to keep an oath. It is futile for sinful humanity to try to keep a covenant with God, because we will always stumble. And it is folly to labor to keep a covenant that has already been kept.

As with all covenants, blood was shed. But in this case the blood came from the One in whom the covenant was made and kept. When the Lord Jesus and His followers gathered in the upper room on the eve of His crucifixion, the disciples didn't realize it but they were celebrating the giving of a New Covenant. The Passover had been a shadow of that which was coming to pass in reality through the shed blood of Jesus, the unblemished Lamb.

When Christians gather at the Lord's table for communion, it is the shared meal sealing the benefits of the New Covenant. It is the symbolic ingesting of the covenant benefits that we have not earned. And could never earn in all eternity.

Oh, behold the crimson vista and let your shame be swallowed up into the all-powerful provision of this New Covenant!

It's not up to you to measure up!

There is no performance left for you to render.

There is no sacrifice left for you to make.

There is no chance that the New Covenant can fail.

Are you in Christ? Then rejoice forevermore. Unless Jesus fails, you cannot be separated from the benefits of the covenant. If Jesus can make it through another night without disobeying the Father, then all the blessings of the New Covenant are yours for another day.

This is the Christian's mountaintop cry—it is finished, it is fulfilled, the Covenant is complete! All who believe it and accept it are in Christ. All who are in Christ are heirs of the covenant blessings!

We do not need to add something to the finished work of Jesus Christ. There is no striving left—only a surrendering! There is no performance expected—just the passion of our gratitude!

When God blesses you, He isn't blessing you because you have done something wonderful, but because His Son has done something wonderful. The faithfulness of God is not faithfulness to a covenant He made with you, but to the covenant He made with the Son.

the ultimate answer to my shame

What does the New Covenant mean to me? It means the answer to my shame! It means that I can be free from the fear of failing or losing God's love. If the covenant is made and kept in Christ, and I am in Christ, then it's a done deal and nothing can separate me from the love of God in Christ Jesus. Nothing can keep me from the full blessing of God except the deception that I must do something more in order to receive it.

What does the New Covenant mean to me? It means that I have a whole new faith. It means that my confidence is not in my ability to have mental certainty of a positive prayer outcome, but in my assurance that Jesus has kept the covenant. For example, if I visit the hospital and pray for a cancer patient to be made well, I no longer put pressure on myself to conjure up some kind of inward assurance that the person will get well if I pray hard enough. Instead, I focus my heart and attention upon the finished work of Jesus. "If You have made and kept the covenant in Christ, O God, then I know that it is by those stripes, not my prayer performance, that we are healed."

What does the New Covenant mean to me? A whole new joy in prayer. The prayer of my life has shifted from "O Lord, bless me," to "O Lord, let the eyes of my heart be enlightened that I might more fully comprehend how blessed I am in Christ Jesus." Instead of primarily praying, "O Lord, change my circumstances," I pray, "Change me so that I do not fall for the shaming lies of the enemy—deceptions that would sabotage my freedom to walk out the spiritual inheritance I have in Christ."

The agony of shame is built upon one simple lie: There is something more that you must do in order to be blessed. The answer to that lie is in the truth of the New Covenant. It is the healing news you've always needed: There is nothing else you must do in order to be blessed. It's all *in Him*.

"Praise be to the God and Father of our Lord Jesus Christ, who has blessed us in the heavenly realms with every spiritual blessing *in Christ*. For he chose us *in him*...*in him* we have redemption.... *In him* we were also chosen.... And you also were included *in Christ*.... God, who is rich in mercy, made us alive *with Christ*.... And God raised us up *with Christ* and seated us *with him* in the heavenly realms *in Christ Jesus*.... For it is by grace you have been saved, through faith—and this not from yourselves, it is the gift of God—not by works...." (Ephesians 1–2, excerpts).

Please park for a while. Read Paul's words again. *In Him*.... Don't dare hurry away from this viewpoint. It is the solution to shame. It is the radiance of the gospel. It is the highest vista we earthbound creatures can reach.

And I wouldn't trade it for an endless picnic on the Blue Ridge Parkway on a perfect October day.

ASK   A Question to Inquire:

Am I living in the power of the New Covenant or is my Christian life just a modified version of the Old Covenant?

BELIEVE   A Principle to Ponder:

"The New Covenant does not hinge upon your faithfulness. It all hangs upon the faithfulness of Jesus Christ. "God is faithful, by whom you were called into the fellowship of His Son, Jesus Christ our Lord" (1 Corinthians 1:9, NKJV). Being a Christian is not about my faithfulness as much as it is about Jesus' faithfulness. I can put my trust in Christ because He said "It is finished."

CHOOSE   A Commitment to Keep:

I choose today to focus on what Christ has done
for me rather than all that I have yet to do for
Him.

PRAY

*Father God, I praise You for Your mysterious
plan revealed. You have made and kept the New
Covenant in my behalf. I cannot add to or take away
from the infinite love You have already shown me.
Give me eyes to see how wide, how deep, how long,
how high is Your love in Christ Jesus. I thank You
that I am in Christ and, therefore, have been blessed
with every spiritual blessing. Let me cease from
my striving and rest in the finished work of Jesus.
Grant me new courage, faith, and joy as
I live as coheir with Christ. AMEN.*

CHAPTER twelve

CHOOSE
YOUR GOD

Bereaved, despairing, and ashamed, a grieving Hebrew widow named Naomi spoke to the widows of her sons.

"Return home, my daughters. Why would you come with me? Am I going to have any more sons, who could become your husbands? Return home, my daughters; I am too old to have another husband. Even if I thought there was still hope for me—even if I had a husband tonight and then gave birth to sons—would you wait until they grew up?... No, my daughters. It is more bitter for me than for you, because the LORD's hand has gone out against me.... Don't call me Naomi.... Call me Mara, because the Almighty has made my life very bitter" (Ruth 1:11–13, 20).

By now you can easily recognize the dynamics of her shame. *"I don't measure up anymore...I'm too old...There's no hope...No one should be around me...May as well change my name to "Bitter," 'cause that's what I am."*

All the shame symptoms are there, aren't they? Feelings

of worthlessness. Negative forecasts. Hopelessness. Isolation. Self-curse.

Naomi had suffered the death of her husband and her sons. Her grief was necessary, but her shame was not. Her grief saddened her, but her shame enslaved her. When we lose that which is precious, we need to grieve, but we need not lose hope. Naomi's shame was blockading all remaining blessing out of her life. Shame will not only dishearten you today, it will also cause you to sabotage the healing that is ready to soothe you.

There was no way that Naomi could just "get over" the loss of her husband and sons. I can only imagine the depth of her triple grief. She would miss them forever. Her life would never be the same. She arouses our pity. She needed unreserved comfort. But there also was a huge error in her heart that needed correction.

Naomi's husband and sons had been given to her as blessings, but unwittingly, she had made them her idols. An idol is anything we set on a pedestal and declare: "You will be my source of life, joy, security, or meaning."

THE MEASURE OF YOUR WORTH

Much of our shame results from our idolatry. Jeremiah prophesied it plainly: "Every goldsmith is shamed by his idols" (Jeremiah 10:14). In our attempts to prop up added security and self-worth in our lives, we cling to people, places, or possessions as the answers for our deep sense of inadequacy and crushing need.

Initially, our idols seem more accessible than Almighty God. They seem less demanding and more manageable than the surrendered life of authentic discipleship.

We become like Naomi, who believed in God, but whose sense of value had become thoroughly enmeshed with the presence of her husband and sons. For Christians, idolatry is not the substitute of one god for another—it's the addition of self-made gods to the one true God. After erecting the idols in our lives in an attempt to manage life and maintain a feeling of happiness, those idols seize control in an opportune moment and turn to mock their makers.

Naomi had made an idol of her husband, but like all the minions of darkness, this idol turned against the idolater and shamed her. The thing that she had counted on to feel valuable, the presence of a good husband and sons, turned against her to mock her worth altogether.

Don't let your worth be measured by anything you make or possess. Let your worth be measured by the One who made you. We are tempted to think that getting more of something will heal our sense of emptiness and inadequacy. Yet the simple truth is that we're more likely to find healing by letting go of something we consider essential.

For example, part of my healing has come through letting go of my deep need for others' approval. If I believe my value depends upon my popularity with people, I will believe that the answer to my shame is to become more popular. I will become a people pleaser. I will devote my energy to winning the approval of others.

Then, if and when I finally obtain the idol of popularity, it momentarily anesthetizes my shame. But it does not heal it. After a momentary "high" from the approval that one person grants me, I will inevitably be put to shame by the disapproval I receive from another. If on Sunday morning five hundred people tell me "Good sermon," but I get one disapproving note, I'll discover the true power of the approval idol in my life.

The reason that we make idols is because we think that we can use them to somehow boost our self-esteem. So I might say to myself, "If I just get enough approval, then I'll know that I measure up and I will finally be able to feel secure and be at peace." In other words, "I'll make an idol called popularity, and it will be my ticket to fulfillment."

Ironically, however, real peace will not come by my obtaining enormous popularity, but by dying to my need for popularity. Real peace comes to me not by gaining your approval, but by no longer needing your approval to feel good about myself. Ultimately, I am not blessed by my idol of popularity but am pressured to always have it. When I do not perform for my idol well enough, it mocks me and sends me back to an even deeper prison of shame.

Naomi's grief could only be healed by the comfort of the Holy Spirit. But only letting go of her idols could heal her shame. Naomi had to accept that while her husband and sons were the most profound blessings in her life, they could not be her gods. In fact, the only way Naomi could be healed of her bitterness was to lose what she had always counted on for her self-worth…and discover that she was valuable anyway.

That's why Ruth's role in the story is so beautiful.

That's why Matthew makes sure we take note that Ruth

was King David's grandmother. That's why Jesus comes from Ruth's line. It is the lineage of those who heal others by being a friend to sinners. Ruth, whose very name means, "friend," did not point Naomi toward a comfortable, idolatrous answer by saying, "Don't worry, Naomi, there will be another man for me and you. You can still find worth in a husband one day." Instead of issuing false promises that reinforced Naomi's idolatry, Ruth loved Naomi and affirmed the best in her.

"Don't urge me to leave you or to turn back from you. Where you go I will go, and where you stay I will stay. Your people will be my people and your God my God" (Ruth 1:16).

Ruth had been drawn to the God she had witnessed in Naomi. In spite of her grief and depression, there was still the glow of the transcendent in Naomi. Though Naomi saw herself as bitterness personified, Ruth saw her as a woman of deep godliness. Though Naomi saw herself as useless and undeserving of companionship, Ruth saw her as the very connection to the meaning of life.

When you've lost everything that you ever depended upon for your sense of self-worth, and someone values you anyway, you begin to suspect that there is something of worth still in you. I can think of nothing more healing than to fail utterly and still be loved. In the midst of such unconditional love, the idols come toppling down and their shame loses its force.

my three idols

In an attempt to feel secure in my broken world, I fashioned at least three idols which, in turn, shamed me. I had committed my life to looking good, sounding smart, and being liked.

I found out early in life that, as the youngest of three boys, I couldn't be as perfect as my oldest brother or as strong as my middle brother, but I *could* be cute.

People like cute.

Cute works.

Nobody kicks a little puppy dog. Even if it poops in the wrong place or chews up a good shoe, you just can't hurt a cute little puppy. As the little one in the family, I learned how to get petted. I talked baby talk to my first grade teacher and she smiled.

I got things by being cute—things like attention, affection, and bigger scoops of ice cream. It worked and so, even though I grew into adulthood, I was still committed to looking good in others' eyes. No, I wasn't still talking baby talk and, no, I've never been obsessed with my physical appearance. But I *was* obsessed with how I appeared to people. I showed the parts of me that people would find attractive and hid the unattractive parts. In short, I depended on developing an attractive personality.

Of course, there's nothing wrong with developing a winsome personality—unless it becomes an idol.

As I grew up, the idol shamed me because I found myself under constant pressure to live up to my own "cute" persona. I feared the rejection that might accompany a more transparent, earthy, and real soul. I was a slave to my own cuteness!

The second idol I erected was sounding smart. I say "sounding" smart because I really didn't care that much about *being* smart. I just wanted to appear that way. I admired people who sounded smart. I figured others would admire me for sounding smart. And to some extent they did.

I developed a lot of my inward sense of security from my ongoing A performance in school. I could speak well. I started entering public speech contests in the seventh grade. When I was "on stage," there was no trace of the personal shyness that actually afflicted my soul so greatly throughout my youth and young adulthood. When I would speak, I singled myself out from the crowd. I was lifted up for my ability to sound smart.

But that idol shamed me, too. Imagine the tyranny of sitting in a schoolroom and feeling like the pressure's on to say something smart. All the time. On demand. Imagine the haunting fear of saying the wrong thing, getting the answer wrong publicly, and letting the world know that you're a fraud. The fear of looking dumb often paralyzed me. One of the best gifts in my life, an articulate voice and pen, became one of shame's greatest tools of torment.

Third, as I've already described, I idolized approval. At least it kept me out of trouble. I didn't want to let anybody down who might disapprove of me in any way. I would try to please the authorities in my life by saying what they wanted to hear. I became a master of knowing how to please people without them knowing that I was trying to please them. People applaud people pleasers. I was applauded, embraced, elevated, and more easily forgiven because of my commitment to keep others happy.

Only later did I realize that my commitment to please people made me constantly vulnerable to bitter roots, which would spring up, exhausting me and defiling others. After a while, you will always resent the people that you are so desperately trying to please. You figure that the constant anxiety in your soul is because of *them*—the people who are so demanding of you. What happens when you can't please someone? What then?

Looking good, sounding smart, pleasing people—those were lifelines to me. I thought that getting more of those Big Three was my avenue to a shame-free life.

Instead, to heal my shame, God had to take those idols away.

The process by which those idols are being destroyed continues—and it *is* a process. As it turned out, the Lord dealt all three of those idols a serious blow in what was certainly the holiest—and the funniest—spiritual experience of my life.

the fall of the "big three"

In 1993, I was minding my own business, pastoring a very nice Presbyterian church with very nice people. Things were just dandy.

But then my mother stepped into the picture with an invitation, and everything changed. She invited (actually insisted) that I visit her church for a meeting that, I was told, would be like Pentecost itself.

Their church had been hosting a Pentecostal evangelist named Richard Moore, who, by various reports, had ushered in a powerful move of God. I was told about signs and wonders like those seen at Pentecost or in the Great Awakenings—shaking, falling, laughing (and other manifestations equally unnerving to a nice, young Presbyterian minister pastoring, did I mention, quite a nice congregation).

I was not comfortable at my mother's church during that season in my life. I was comfortable at my Presbyterian church. It felt good...like an old slipper. Besides, I already considered myself filled with the Spirit. I affirmed the gifts of the Holy Spirit and was happy for anyone who had a meaningful experience of God's power. But I knew that those Pentecostal meetings did not provide a safe environment for my reliable three—looking good, sounding smart, and pleasing people.

In the first place, if you shake or fall or roll around on a church floor, you don't look cool at all. Second, if you laugh uncontrollably or speak in strange, undecipherable sounds, you don't sound smart. And third, if I did any of the above, word would surely leak back to my nice Presbyterian congregation...whereupon my approval rating would drop drastically.

Respectable Presbyterian pastors just don't do "those things."

My mother, however, is a very persistent lady. I finally went, just because she wouldn't stop asking. When the meeting was just about over, I had to admit that it seemed real enough. People were amazingly joyful. And the people who fell down didn't seem to be faking it. It had been a long meeting, it was an interesting experience, but mainly, I had done it— now my mom would stop pestering me.

Just before my wife and I were about to leave, the young evangelist called out: "I understand that there is a Presbyterian minister and his wife here tonight." It was no supernatural word of knowledge—my mom had tipped off the associate who had ratted to the evangelist. Later, that evangelist would become one of my dearest friends. But that night I trembled just to get close to him.

We were stuck. We had to go up for prayer in front of everyone.

Before we knew what was happening—something happened. I was touched. Filled with peace and joy.

The experience was so wonderful that I dared to go back the next night. Seeing "Brother Presbyterian" in the crowd, the evangelist called me up to tell my testimony of how the Lord had touched me the night before. I was willing. I knew how to stand in front of a crowd and tell a story. Hey, I was a *pastor*. I knew how to look good. Sound smart. Have the whole big crowd liking me.

I stood to speak. The evangelist held the microphone in front of my mouth and asked, "Brother Presbyterian, what happened to you last night?"

What happened next was, well, so outlandish that it almost beggars my belief to write it. But I assure you, it is 100 percent true. I opened my mouth to speak and *no words would come out.*

I was struck dumb! I had thoughts, but could generate no words. Not even one. When I tried to speak, I could only stammer and say, "uuuuh, uuuuh." So much for Idol #2—sounding smart.

After allowing an extended period of my mute humiliation, the evangelist laughed and said, "Well, that's a fine testimony." He then playfully popped me on the belly with his hand and said, "Filled." When he did so, it was like electricity jolted through my entire body and I was thrust backward to the ground. Uncontrollably, I shook, I laughed, and then I began to cry. I then became like a frozen person, unaware of my surroundings, unconscious of time.

Later, I was told, I rested frozen-like on the steps of that church chancel for over an hour while the evangelist preached his sermon, took up an offering, and prayed for hundreds of people. For over an hour, I was on my back in front of about a thousand people. So much for Idol #1—looking good.

While I lay there, mute, weeping, crying, and shaking, I felt something strange rising up in my spirit. When I finally could speak, only three words would come. I don't know if they were spoken in an audible whisper or were silently reverberating in my spirit. But I will never forget those three words. They were the answer to the third idol in my life.

"I don't care. I don't care. I don't care."

I repeated them over and over and over. For more than an hour. What I meant, of course, was that for once in my life I didn't care what people thought. The experience that had overtaken me was so real, so loving, so powerful, and so healing that I didn't care who saw me. That part of me that wanted to pull myself off that floor, slink down in a chair, and hide from sight lest people see Brother Presbyterian looking quite undignified and, even worse, having word leak back to my own congregation, was overwhelmed. Some new part of me took ascendancy—a part that cared more for the sweet presence and fellowship of God than for the approval of others. Suddenly, the whole needing-to-be-liked reflex that's followed me all of my life seemed an utterly insignificant token compared to the reward of this intimate encounter with Jesus Christ.

At least for those moments, I just didn't care about what others thought. Down came Idol #3, and in came a new freedom.

Of course, the dethroning of my idols didn't happen all at

once that night, but it certainly began there. And I began to find healing from my shame. Shame cannot be healed until what you've always relied upon for your sense of security and worth is stripped away, and you discover God's grace to be altogether better.

It's time to let go of your idols.

IDENTIFYING YOUR IDOLS

How can you identify your idols? It's as simple as filling in the blanks.

If I only could _____, then I would feel good about myself.

If I only had _____, then I would be at peace.

If only _____, then I would no longer be ashamed.

I wish I could say that my freedom came just as easily as taking the idol off the shelf and tossing it out the back door. But honestly, dismantling a long-standing idol isn't usually that simple. We develop deep strongholds in our thinking that must be reversed. Addictions that pull at us emotionally, mentally, and chemically. Unhealthy relationships that enmesh us.

Destroying an idol can feel a lot like death. After all, if the lifeline you've always counted on for personal ego or comfort is suddenly gone, it leaves your soul crying out for help.

That empty cry of the soul is so vulnerable and frightening that most people dare not allow themselves into it. Most people cling to their idols for their whole lives so that they will not have to face that soul cry. And most people who dare to topple their idols face enormous temptation to erect the false gods again—because it tastes like a death to all that feels normal. If you've spent your whole life trying to perform so that others approve of you, it seems almost unimaginable to let go of it—especially if you've been good at it.

That's why, unfortunately, most people don't let go until their idols are yanked away from them. Or they have hit a rock bottom so deep that the pain of keeping the idol outweighs the pain of letting it go.

Life is like a flight on the high trapeze. Swinging on that high bar isn't what's difficult. Most of us, especially us high achievers, can swing to some amazing heights, holding on with all our might.

What's difficult is letting go.

It's difficult because every instinct within us wants to hold on. It seems altogether unnatural to let go of a sure thing in order to embrace a possible thing. And like the high trapeze act, when I let go of my high swing, the other swing has not yet quite arrived. I have to trust that it will arrive in the nick of time and that I'll be able to take hold of that new swing. I have to also trust that the new swing will carry me to a more glorious height.

How will you find the courage to let go of your idols?

I suggest that you begin by asking yourself a question. *Have they worked?* I mean, has whatever you've sought—popularity, promiscuity, perfection—brought you lasting relief from the pressure of life? Have your idols introduced peace into your heart or have they, in the end, made your heart troubled? Have your idolatrous pursuits—drugs, shopping, overeating—brought you abundant life?

At some point in my life, I realized my idols were big lies. Nothing more than fantasies—mirages on the desert of life's landscape.

A friend for whom I've prayed for a year and a half surrendered his heart to God recently. Our stories are virtually the same—alcoholic homes, overachieving goals. Without God, he took the path of cocaine. He was deeply addicted. The first month at a recovery center didn't work—he started using again shortly after he was out. But now that he's surrendered to the true God, he recognizes that cocaine is a false god.

Yesterday he had his first major temptation. He was visiting a friend when the drug man showed up and the alcohol began to flow. Before, he would have lied to himself. He would have said, "It won't hurt—this one time won't set me back. It'll feel good. I'll be all right; it won't ruin my recovery."

But this time he ran. With all his might. He made a two and a half-hour drive in one and a half hours, got back in town, and made it to a Narcotics Anonymous meeting.

"What enabled you to resist?" I asked him. "How has your thinking changed?"

His answer was simple. "Now I play the tape all the way through in my mind. Before, I would just play the first part of the tape—how good the 'high' would feel. The euphoria, the sex, the feeling of freedom. But I never used to play the rest of the tape. That's the part where your wife is packing her bags, your car is being taken away by the repo man on his truck, you're filing bankruptcy, and you can't wake up in the morning. Now," he said, "I play the whole tape through. I remember the hell of the second half of that tape."

"It reminds me," I told him, "of the Hebrew Passover meal. Every part of the meal is symbolic including the bitter herbs. Faithful Jews eat bitter things in the midst of the feast because it's essential never to forget the bitterness of slavery."

"It's slavery, all right," he said. "I don't want to go back to that slavery again."

So ask yourself, "Has it worked?" Have your idols liberated you or enslaved you? Play the tape all the way through. I assure you, the idols that promise to make you feel good will, in the end, shame you. And their mocking laughter will reverberate in the halls of hell. Seeing that your idols don't work is the first step to letting them go.

Letting Go

Still, how can you know that the next swing of your high trapeze will be there? If you let go of your false gods, how can you know there will be a true God who will be present and ready to accept you? That's another way of asking, how can you believe in a God that you can neither see nor touch?

If this letting go of the old begins with seeing the hellishness of idolatry, it continues with the deep suspicion that there must be a better way. If my first question is about your idolatry, *Has it worked?*, my second question is about your longing, *Don't you hunger for something more?*

There is a design at work in the universe that proves an amazing consistency between my longings and the realities available to fulfill those longings. If I feel lonely and long for companionship, then it must be that such a thing as intimacy exists. If I feel thirsty, it proves that there must be a thing called water to satisfy my thirst. If I long for love in an ultimate sense, real love must exist. If I long for Someone who does not love me because I perform but just because I am, that Someone must live somewhere.

And so He does.

When you reach out toward God, you aren't reaching out blindly; you are responding to the deepest desire of your soul. You aren't reaching out into unreality; you are reaching out *because* of the reality of your inmost hunger.

Still, perhaps you say to me, *It's just too scary. I can't let go until I'm sure that His love is there. What can I do?*

If that is your question, I have good news. You don't have to let go in order to discover that God loves you. In fact, everything that makes the good news good is summed up in this: "This is love: not that we loved God, but that He loved us" (1 John 4:10).

God doesn't love you because you let go of your idols—He already loves you. In the end, God is not like the next bar of the trapeze swinging out to you over a chasm. Instead, God is more like the expert trapeze artist who meets you in midair, catches you in His strong grip, and swings you to a safe platform. Never mind that there's no net below, because He will never, never let you go.

But you have to let go of the old bar first. "I have you in My arms," He says. "You can't fall. When I give the word, just let go. I'll catch you and carry you to a new height."

"You see, at just the right time, when we were still powerless, Christ died for the ungodly. Very rarely will anyone die for a righteous man, though for a good man someone might possibly dare to die. But God demonstrates his own love for us in this: While we were still sinners, Christ died for us" (Romans 5:6–8).

God doesn't love you because you can destroy your idols. You can destroy your idols because God *already* loves you. God's love isn't the reward for our repentance; it is the power that makes our repentance possible.

More than I know that food or water exists, I know that God is there, because He has satisfied my deepest longings. Unlike every other world religion or spiritual practice, the gospel of Jesus Christ is not about religious performance. In fact, it's not a religion at all. It's a love relationship. It is there, in the arms of that love relationship, that I have found the answer to my shame.

Only there, in the strong embrace of God's Son, have I found any real rest from inward drivenness. Only there, in the radiance of the Savior's smiling face, have I found any lasting sense of acceptance. Only there, in the strength of my Lord's mighty outstretched hand, have I ever felt truly safe.

Here is perhaps the greatest irony of life: You might love your idols, but they do not love you. You might *not* love God, but He *does* love you. You might serve your idols, but they will always ultimately fail you. You might *not* serve God, but He will never fail *you*. Nothing you can do will ever add or detract from the love that God has demonstrated for you.

The whole Christian message hinges upon this: God loves

you so much that He came in the flesh, in the person of Jesus Christ, to die in your place. Once you've died for someone, you can't show any greater or lesser love. Life isn't about measuring up to someone's standard, not even God's. Life is about receiving and giving love. So if God loves you—*shame off you*. If God is for you, who could be against you?

In the end, I must admit, my shame is not the product of the wounds of my past, but of the idols I have established in an effort to salve those wounds. I encourage you to make the same simple admission, because in it is an assurance of profound hope. If it's true that my shame is not ultimately someone else's fault, then it must also be true that I am not ultimately a victim. Shame will have no more hold over my life than the status I grant to my idols.

No matter what wounds, mistakes, or failures haunt you, your past is not the determining power in your life. In the end, even if you have suffered deep abuse, your abusers do not have the say over the health of your soul. You can make choices today that dethrone the very idols that continue to shame you. Most importantly, you can surrender to the expansive love of Father God and let Him take the shame off you.

ASK   A Question to Inquire:

What are my idols?

BELIEVE   A Principle to Ponder:

"Do not let your worth be measured by anything you make. Let your worth be measured by the One who made you. We are tempted to think that getting more of something will heal our shame. Ironically, however, our shame is more likely to be healed by letting go of something we consider essential."

We erect idols because we believe they will give us security and fulfillment, but instead, they shame us further. When my idols are abolished and I surrender to the one true God, I am set free and discover joy.

CHOOSE   A Commitment to Keep:

I choose today to identify and renounce the idols I have made so that God alone will have dominion over my life.

PRAY

O Lord, there is no other God but You. You alone are the Creator of the ends of the earth. You alone are the Lifegiver. You alone are the Healer. You alone are the hope of the world. Let no false god rule in the hidden places of my heart. Forgive me for every idol that I have made, and grant me the courage to tear them down from their lofty places in my life. Take me in Your arms, assure me of my safety in You, and carry me to the new heights I know You have destined for me. In Jesus' name, AMEN.

**For the *Shame Off You* Workbook
or audio series,
visit
www.alanwright.org**

Notes

1. *Winston-Salem Journal*, C1, 8 2003.
2. Adapted from Patrick J. Carnes, *Don't Call It Love* (New York: Bantam Books, 1991), 102–103.
3. See Larry Crabb, *The Silence of Adam* (Grand Rapids, MI: Zondervan Publishing House, 1995).
4. Gordon Dalbey, unpublished article.
5. John Calvin, *Institutes of the Christian Religion* (Philadelphia: Westminster Press, 1960), 35.
6. Dudley Hall, *Grace Works* (Sisters, OR: Multnomah Publishers, Inc., 2000), 168.
7. Most of the literature refers to two types of shame: healthy shame and unhealthy (sometimes called corrosive or toxic) shame (see, for example, Lewis B. Smedes, *Shame and Grace*, HarperSanFrancisco, 1993). Sandra Wilson refers to three varieties of shame: biological, biblical, and binding shame (*Released from Shame*, Intervarsity Press, 1990). Healthy shame, or in Wilson's words, biblical shame, is what I term "conviction." I prefer the word *conviction*, not only for simplicity but also because it is the biblical word for the work of the Holy Spirit in leading us to repentance (John 16:8).
8. A sermon title shared with me in personal conversations with Rev. Stanley Bennett.
9. Dudley Hall, *Grace Works*, 152–53.
10. Paul Tournier, *Guilt and Grace: A Psychological Study* (New York: Harper and Row Publishers, 1962), 175.
11. Gordon Dalbey, unpublished article.
12. Dudley Hall, *Grace Works*, 18.
13. Precisely what Paul asserts in Romans 1:19–20.
14. See 1 Kings 18, Elijah versus the prophets of Baal.

A CHILDLIKE HEART

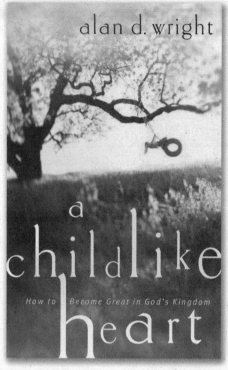

1-57673-719-5

To all of us too-serious, on-the-edge, busy-and-preoccupied adults, Alan Wright offers a reminder of Jesus' words regarding the heart of the child: "Of such is the kingdom of God." In this paperback edition of *A Childlike Heart*, Wright reveals how we can recapture the unbridled freedom we once relished. As we look back with nostalgia and appreciation at the simple pleasures of our growing-up years, Wright explains, we will rediscover how our days can be characterized by a spirit of adventure and wide-eyed joy in the Lord.

www.multnomah.net